OVERCOMING LONELINESS

OVERCOMING LONELINESS

W. LESLIE CARTER
PAUL D. MEIER
FRANK B. MINIRTH

Published by Fleming H. Revell
a division of Baker Book House Company
P.O. Box 6287, Grand Rapids, MI 49516-6287

Spire edition published 2000

Printed in the United States of America

ISBN 0-8007-8689-0

For current information about all releases from Baker Book House, visit our web site:

http://www.bakerbooks.com

To
our colleagues through the years
at our counseling clinics.
You have been a tremendous encouragement
and an integral part of our success.

CONTENTS

INTRODUCTION

WHAT ARE THE SYMPTOMS, causes, and cures of loneliness? There is an even more basic question: What is loneliness? And how does one attain emotional intimacy? We have attempted to answer these and other questions in this book.

Certainly the symptoms of loneliness are rampant in America today. In fact, these symptoms have become much of the background theme of country-western music—the fastest-growing segment of the entertainment industry. We have attempted to outline not only the obvious symptoms, but also the subtle ones, so that the reader can answer questions he or she may have; for example, "Why do I feel lonely?" "How lonely am I?" "What can I do about it?"

Other questions logically follow. "What causes loneliness: Is it primarily rejection by others, my own fears, faulty parenting, or society itself?" "Is loneliness inevitable or is there something I can do to attain emotional intimacy in its place?" "Is attaining emotional intimacy worth the effort?"

We have attempted to outline practical steps for attaining emotional intimacy. With tongue in cheek, we have devoted our first chapter to teaching ways one can *avoid* intimacy if one is afraid of it for some reason. We have drawn on our knowledge of medicine, psychiatry, and theology to write this book, but we have also drawn from both our own personal experiences with loneliness and our own struggles to achieve emotional intimacy.

We wish to thank our clinic secretaries, Nancy Brown, Robin Henderson, Judy Moreland, Jeanne Ryan, and Vicky Warren, for their help to us and each other in making the time and effort to get this book typed and corrected.

LES CARTER
PAUL MEIER
FRANK MINIRTH

For further information regarding the nationwide services of the Minirth-Meier Clinic, please call 1-888-MINIRTH.

PART I

A PORTRAIT OF LONELINESS

ONE

INTIMACY AND HOW TO AVOID IT!

People Who Avoid Intimacy

SINCE MOST OF THIS BOOK is devoted to helping the majority of its readers learn about the causes of loneliness and ways to attain intimacy, it seems only fair to devote one chapter to those few who don't want to get close to others. There are many semivalid reasons why some people choose to avoid intimacy. For instance, when they were growing up, they may have been scarred emotionally by their parents. As preschoolers, they may have tried to get close to either Mom or Dad or both but felt pushed off. Mom and Dad may have had a variety of emotional insecurities of their own and therefore chose to avoid intimacy with their preschoolers, managing to stay too busy to listen to their children's feelings. After all, doesn't society teach us that "children should be seen and not heard"?

Others have reached out to their peers for intimacy and felt bitterly rejected for a variety of reasons. These unfortunate humans believe they have a right to protect themselves from the pain of further rejection by using whatever techniques are available to them to avoid intimacy with other people.

A third category avoid intimacy because they don't like themselves very much! They often think to themselves, "If my acquaintances could only read my thoughts and know what I am really like, they would almost certainly reject me!" We have a special empathy for this group, because many of them would prefer to have the joy of intimacy but feel they don't deserve it. They have to choose between, on the one hand, pursuing intimacy (or at least a superficial intimacy) and feeling guilty about it (since they aren't good enough), and, on the other, avoiding intimacy while maintaining a clear conscience. Many humans make the latter choice.

A fourth category of people who frequently avoid intimacy consists of those who have been taught that *all* humans (themselves included) are worthless. Their parents constantly talked about how bad everybody was and how terrible every situation was. Then, for reinforcement, they went to churches that preached hellfire and damnation every single Sunday, except for an occasional lecture on man's total sinfulness. Who wants to get intimate with such worthless creatures?

For these and other reasons, a few readers may choose to skip the rest of this book on intimacy and how to attain it and just study this first chapter to learn some new ways of being an introvert (or a superficially friendly extrovert) and avoiding intimacy with all its dangers. Those readers who do want to meet their three basic needs (intimacy with God, others, and self), we encourage to go ahead and study this chapter anyway. It will give you a much better understanding of and empathy for lonely people. It will also help you understand how and why so many people who are important to you have avoided becoming intimate with you, parents included in some cases. You may have naively thought it was your own fault that they avoided intimacy with you, when in reality it was their problem based on their past painful experiences. Finally, it is our hope that, after studying this book, you may even learn to *love* lonely people, as we have.

Ways to Avoid Intimacy

Workaholism

A very common and seemingly moral way to avoid intimacy with one's mate and children is to become a workaholic. In fact, we see this problem so often at our psychiatric clinic that several of us wrote a book entitled *The Workaholic and His Family* (Baker).

The most likely candidate for workaholism is the oldest son or daughter of demanding parents. This is especially true if acceptance by his or her parents was conditional on meeting their unreasonably high expectations. In such a family environment, one learns rapidly to suppress emotions and strive for perfectionism in a computerlike fashion. All early-childhood attempts at finding emotional intimacy with one's parents are met with painful rejection and criticism. Thus, avoiding intimacy becomes an early-childhood decision.

A perfectionist from this kind of background can misinterpret the pain of loneliness as being a punishment he deserves for not achieving enough to please his parents. Thus, rather than seeking intimacy with God, his mate, children, peers, and himself, the perfectionist seeks greater and greater financial, academic, political, or social achievements. He works eighty to one hundred hours a week to prove his significance (but never quite proves it) and uses the Protestant work ethic as a moralistic excuse for not meeting his family's needs for emotional intimacy. Thus, one can be a financial, academic, political, or social success while maintaining superficial relationships with God and peers and sinning grossly against God by not meeting the emotional needs of one's family. Not a bad way of avoiding intimacy, considering the other options.

Sports Fanaticism

Being a sports fanatic is a fun way to avoid intimacy. We have often used it ourselves and enjoyed it. Now there is nothing wrong with loving and enjoying sports, of course, unless sports-related activities are interfering with the high priority of meeting one's own intimacy needs and the intimacy needs of one's mate and children. Some men watch sports on television for as much as twenty hours a week while ignoring their wife and children. Some women jog, play tennis, or are involved in some other form of sports activities many hours a week while neglecting their mate and children.

Substituting Sex for Intimacy

Learning to substitute sex for intimacy is easy since it is reinforced over and over again in our society. Just observe what happens in soap operas, in the movies, or even with your neighbors. Or consider a Kenny Rogers song that celebrates the good feeling that comes from picking up various women in bars. When describing the great sensation that comes from such experiences, Kenny sings out, "And I think it's love."

One of the most effective ways to avoid true human emotional intimacy is to confuse yourself into believing what the world so often teaches, that sexual pleasure is love (emotional intimacy), or that the crushes you have on certain individuals are love. This is a rather stupid thing to believe, but there are countless people who believe it.

Let's see what lies behind this confusion of sex with intimacy. Any human who does not have enough emotional intimacy (true love with God, others, and self) will suffer from a gnawing emotional pain. A mature human will recognize this vacuum for what it is and do whatever is necessary to develop better relationships with God, others, and self. An immature person will think this gnawing discomfort is someone else's fault, or a physical illness, or a need for material things, for power (control), or for sex. Substituting sex for intimacy becomes relatively easy if one convinces himself (or herself) that the pain of loneliness is really his (or her) sex drive. He will then develop a crush on someone of the opposite sex who subconsciously reminds him of his parent of the opposite sex.

Here is an example. A movie actress whom we recently treated was very depressed and lonely. Well practiced in substituting sex for intimacy, she was in the process of divorcing her fifth husband. All of her husbands were sociopathic personalities who had totally controlled her and beaten her whenever they thought she was out of line. We surmised that her father must have been a controlling, sociopathic man who beat her when she was growing up. She was surprised that we had guessed correctly, since she had never mentioned her father. She was even more surprised when we asked how old she was when her father had first abused her sexually. She had never told anyone this deep, hidden secret and was surprised that we could have guessed it. We explained to her that she had an intense craving for the emotional intimacy which she wanted but never received from her father, and that she was misinterpreting this craving as a sexual need. Therefore she developed crushes on father-substitutes. All five of the men she "fell in love with" were sociopaths who, like her father, were considerably older than she and abused her.

When all this was explained to the actress, she became angry at our insinuation that she was not in total control of her behavior. Within three days she developed a crush on a male patient in the psychiatry ward. And, quite predictably, he was a sociopathic, controlling male who had beaten his wife. Wise King Solomon said three thousand years ago that "as a dog returneth to his vomit, so a fool returneth to his folly" (Prov. 26:11 KJV; see also 2 Peter 2:22).

The main problem with substituting sex for intimacy is that it doesn't work, but most people don't let a little thing like that stop them. A sexual affair brings temporary relief but long-term heartaches and guilt. Although the gnawing pain of loneliness continues, the individual erroneously convinces himself that he is at least doing something about it. However, God intended for sex to be the icing on the cake of marital emotional intimacy—not the cake itself.

Going to Bed at Different Times

How many married couples have you met, one of whom claims to be a "night person" and the other a "morning person"? A night person is someone who is groggy in the morning but comes alive and is wide-awake at night. A morning person is someone who rises early each morning, wide awake and alert, ready to do his or her best work, but winds down at about 9:30 every night. Part of this syndrome is biological (circadian rhythms, biorhythms, pineal gland, etc.), but we are convinced that most of it is psychological. This has a bearing on why many couples seem to have one morning person and one night person.

Let us explain. All humans have some degree of fear of intimacy. Most of us adults consciously want to be emotionally intimate with our mates, but unconsciously we have fears about becoming intimate. We could become overly dependent on our mate to think for us, for example. Or our mate could (and eventually will) die. Or our mates might see us as we really are and, as a result, reject us emotionally or sexually. They might even divorce us. A great many painful things can happen if we become too close to our mates. Therefore, we all use various techniques to keep them at a comfortable distance.

One technique is to go to bed at different times. After discovering that our mate is a morning person or a night person, we may conveniently (but subconsciously, of course!) choose to become the opposite. The body is able to readjust its biological rhythms to habitual behavior patterns. If our mate likes to go to bed early every night so as to get up at 6:00 to jog every morning, we can develop a taste for Johnny Carson or night movies. Or we may get so wrapped up in a book that we can't put it down until it is finished. So our mate goes to bed at 10:00 and we go to bed at 12:30; our mate rises at 6:00 and we wake up around 7:30, drag ourself out of bed, skip breakfast, and trudge wearily off to work. This is an excellent technique for avoiding emotional intimacy, since some of the best times to share intimate feelings are at night in bed when one's inhibitions are lowered during that twenty minutes or so prior to falling asleep. Going to bed at different times also has the added advantage of ruining one's sex life or keeping an already dull sex life from improving (which would result, of course, in greater intimacy).

Separate Bedrooms

Very few people have the nerve to demand separate bedrooms. But if you are rich enough to have an extra bedroom, and if you are neurotically selfish, this method of avoiding intimacy does work. You may wish to try it, especially if other methods have failed to distance you enough from your mate. All you have to do is tell your mate his snoring keeps you awake. Or tell him that he moves around too much at night and kicks and wakes you up. Or if you and your mate are already going to bed at different times, separate bedrooms to avoid waking each other up at 12:30 or 6:00 in the morning is just one step further.

We have counseled scores of couples who have separate bedrooms, and none of them has had emotional intimacy or a good sex life. Our experience indicates that this is an excellent way to avoid intimacy. The major problem with it is that it doubles or triples the likelihood of sexual affairs and eventual divorce, which could hurt your pride and your financial security. So this method of avoiding intimacy is potentially dangerous, even though it works so well. Another disadvantage is that you have to prepare good excuses for avoiding more practical options, such as a king-size bed, twin beds, or ear plugs. A final consequence of separate bedrooms will be perpetuation of your own neuroticism in your children. And in particular, allowing a child to sleep with each mate at different times is sure to result in confusion of sex roles.

Sarcasm

Sarcasm is a slightly more benign method of avoiding intimacy. It's quite simple as well. All you have to do is become as intimate with your mate as you want to. Then, whenever you feel a little bit too close for comfort, use subtle (or obvious) sarcasm with him to make him back off. When he accuses you of being hostile or of making him back off (if he happens to be that insightful, an unlikely possibility), all you have to do is ask, "What's the matter with you? Can't you take a joke?" This gets the blame off your neck (where it belongs) and puts it on his back, a procedure that usually works. Whether or not your mate accepts your accusation that he is being paranoid, the worst thing that can happen is that your mate will come back with some sarcasm of his own to get even with you. This will push you a little further away from emotional intimacy with him. Since this was your original goal, sarcasm is an excellent technique. While making use of it to avoid intimacy, you can look innocent and, with very little effort on your part, become a "victim" of your mate's paranoid revenge.

Having an Affair and Confessing It

Far more complex than substituting sex for intimacy, having an affair and confessing it is a very subtle and devious procedure. Anyone who adopts this procedure must have enough in the way of hysterical (histrionic) personality traits to fool himself into not realizing exactly what it is he is doing. Very few people would plot out this strategy in advance. However, we see it being used over and over again, especially among religious, church-going people.

As an illustration of this complex syndrome, consider the following scenario: Imagine that you had an unsatisfactory relationship with your parent of the opposite sex. You have always craved that parent's emotional affection (since you never received any intimacy from that parent). Then you marry someone very similar to that parent (in the expectation that your mate will become a parent-substitute—besides, all your life you have been used to your parent's personality quirks and any change would be frightening). Unconsciously your anger is transferred from your parent to your mate. Again unconsciously you decide to get even with your parent, through your mate, by offering several years of marriage with very little or no emotional or sexual intimacy.

A few years into your marriage you develop a strong crush on another adult who reminds you of your parent of the opposite sex. You convince yourself unconsciously that you are in love with that person. There are verbal expressions of affection, but at first religious convictions prevent an affair. The situation gradually becomes more and more involved, however, eventually culminating in an affair of some duration. You may have a few twinges of guilt, but not as many as you thought you would have because you have suppressed your feelings of true guilt (for a discussion of guilt see page 113).

As time passes, however, there develops a sense of guilt for not feeling more guilty, so you let yourself get in touch with your guilt. Eventually the feeling of guilt becomes overwhelming, so you go confess to your pastor, who advises you to forsake the affair totally and at once, to confess it to God, and to forgive yourself. He also warns you never to tell your mate. Nonetheless, you feel obligated to tell your mate. Although you may fool yourself into thinking you must tell your mate because of your overwhelming guilt and a need for honesty, there are several less noble and more compelling reasons lying just beneath the surface:

You wish to punish your parent of the opposite sex through hurting your mate.

You can also punish your parent through hurting the person with whom you had the affair, for on learning of the affair, your mate will likely seek revenge by ruining the other party's reputation for having seduced you in the first place.

Several additional years of little or no emotional or sexual intimacy with your mate will be guaranteed, since it takes the average godly mate this long to totally forgive and rebuild a degree of trust. Your mate will *never*, as you know, forget what happened.

So you go ahead and tell your mate, even though your pastor advised you not to. To your surprise, your mate responds by doing all the things your pastor warned you would happen. But you are also gratified that you have accomplished the three less than noble goals listed above. On the advice of your mate and pastor you agree to a year or so of weekly marriage counseling. Although you ignore all of the insights your marriage counselor tries to impart, you do give up the affair and go back to the superficial marriage because all of the subtle, complex, unconscious goals of this whole procedure have been attained, and you can rest assured that there won't be any emotional intimacy to worry about for a long time.

Countering Your Mate's Personality

Countering your mate's personality is a far simpler method of avoiding intimacy. In fact, you can do this consciously. If your mate is an extrovert (a person who likes to be with friends most of the time), then you can become an introvert (a person who enjoys being alone and doesn't like to get together much with friends). If your mate is an introvert, you can become more of an extrovert. The simple solution, of course, would be for you and your mate to compromise: to spend some time with friends, some time with each other, and some time alone. But this would build intimacy, so many people manage to overlook this simple solution.

In countering each other's personality, you and your mate will develop different sets of friends and different social lifestyles. In that way you will avoid developing too much emotional intimacy with each other.

Becoming More Religious

Becoming more religious is a fairly complex means of avoiding intimacy since it can be either conscious or unconscious. One way of proceeding is to commit your life to Christ, but rather than obeying God's Word and becoming more intimate with God, others, and self, you become overzealous about church work instead. This might entail volunteering for multiple positions, or attending the meetings of several church organizations every week. In this way you will keep so busy serving God that you won't have time to meet the needs of your mate and children for intimacy.

Another possibility is to develop a self-righteous attitude. You could preach or witness to your mate in a condescending manner and avoid trying to win your mate to Christ by loving example. You could also make a point of registering disappointment in your mate for not being as holy as you are.

Ignoring Your Mate

One of the simplest ways to avoid intimacy and perhaps the most honest and least guilt-producing is just to ignore your mate. Live together in the same home in a superficial, roommate-like relationship, but avoid all emotional intimacy. Develop separate lives, but be seen together just enough (at church, at PTA meetings, etc.) to maintain your public image. This technique has a great many advantages. In addition to avoiding intimacy, you will also avoid arguments and divorce. By maintaining your public image as a loving married couple, you will keep both sets of in-laws from interfering and will qualify for leadership positions in the church. Moreover, you will maintain financial security since living together is less expensive than living apart. Your children will be able to live with both parents and will naively think that you and your mate have a good relationship since they never see you argue with each other.

Finally, you will both have the freedom to live your own life without being controlled by the other.

In counseling lonely people at our psychiatric clinics, we have seen scores of techniques that people use over and over again to avoid intimacy. In this chapter we have listed ten very common conscious and unconscious techniques. The reader will probably be able to think of more.

Of course, the goal of this chapter is *not* for anyone to actually use these techniques to avoid intimacy. Rather we have employed a little irony in order to expose the stupid games all humans (including ourselves) play to avoid intimacy. The real key to understanding human psychology is found in Jeremiah 17:9: "The heart is deceitful above all things, and desperately wicked: who can know it?" (KJV). Only by catching ourselves using these subtle, deceitful techniques and by *choosing* to make practical behavioral changes with God's help can we attain the great pleasure that comes from emotional intimacy.

TWO

A PERSONAL STRUGGLE

LES CARTER

LONELINESS IS A FACT OF LIFE! As long as we are mortal humans we will be faced with it. Each of us will struggle with it at some point in our lives. One of the basic conditions of humanity is that each of us frequently comes face to face with loneliness. Some people seem to handle it adequately while others feel swallowed up by it.

Loneliness is felt in many different ways. It could be the pain of the individual living alone. It could be the sense of failure that follows an unhappy experience. Or it could come when a person feels painfully aware of his inability to relate to people in a way that brings real satisfaction. Although it would be splendid if we could simply ignore it and wait for it to go away, we are only kidding ourselves if we do so.

This book will reveal many ways in which loneliness enters our lives. It will also emphasize that we can win consistent victories over loneliness. No one ever truly wants to feel lonely. Sometimes we may want to be alone, but that is not the same as feeling lonely. Our task together will be to explore the reasons why loneliness exists, the way it influences our lives, and how we can overcome it. Since everyone has an instinctual desire to grow, each of us has the potential to actively seek out ways of working through our emotional problems. With a God-given strength, as we grow to understand the problem of loneliness, we can minimize and neutralize its effects on our lives.

I wish I could tell you that I have never had to struggle with loneliness. But that would not be truthful. Because of my humanness I have been confronted with it many times. I have known the loneliness that comes after having misunderstandings with friends and family members. I have known the loneliness that results from personal rejection. I have experienced the lonely feeling that accompanies the responsibility of having to be the bearer of bad news to people dear to me. In spite of my study and knowledge of human emotions, I will never be completely immune to the ill effects of loneliness.

But I realize that it is in my own best interest to learn to cope with and minimize the lonely experiences in life that come my way. In doing so, my relationship with God will be strengthened, my relationships with those around me will become more rewarding, and I will learn to appreciate myself more.

Perhaps my greatest bout with loneliness came in connection with a major accident that occurred fairly recently in my life. For a while, my entire lifestyle was severely jolted, and I had several different trying situations to face.

For several months I had been working very hard. In my counseling practice, the workload was heavy and I kept a tight schedule with my clients. I would find myself wanting time to slow down and rest, but not really getting it. When I was away from work, I was presenting seminars, writing articles, trying to sell my house in order to move into a new one. I needed a break.

My big chance for a rest came when my wife and I were invited to spend an extended weekend with some friends at a lake cabin. There would be no phones, no appointments, no pressing responsibilities. My wife and I had an ideal chance to spend some quality time with each other and with our friends. It was "just what the doctor had ordered." My only work was to be in charge of the barbecue we had planned (one of my favorite pastimes). As the weekend progressed, I became truly relaxed and content.

But then came the accident. While at the lake, we had access to a motorboat, which we used for water skiing. It had been several years since I had enjoyed this sport, and I felt young and carefree out on the lake. On the second full day of the weekend, while on the skis, I wound up running into some tree stumps. I took a terrible spill and suffered injuries far worse than I had ever had before.

Near death, I was rushed by paramedics to the nearest hospital for emergency care. The doctors found that both of my legs, my pelvis, and my right arm were broken. In addition, there were a large loss of blood and some internal injuries to my bladder and lungs. I spent the next five days in the critical-care unit and a total of eight weeks in the hospital.

Talk about having to make some adjustments! This was the sort of accident that I never expected to happen to me. To someone else, maybe, but not me. Yet, there I was, after four operations, all banged up and disabled. I had known of other people who had to cope with serious setbacks. But this time I was the one who had to cope with an unwanted situation.

At first, somewhat surprisingly, I had very little difficulty in accepting the conditions that had befallen me. Support and encouragement came pouring in from family, friends, and acquaintances. People that I had never met came by my side to offer any help possible. Members of my immediate family were particularly helpful in taking time away from their normal routines to minister to my needs and those of my wife. I had a strong faith in God, which helped me sustain hope that He would take this calamity and use it for my personal growth.

Yet as time wore on, even in the face of such faith, support, and encouragement, I was unable to completely escape the feelings of discouragement and depression. Though I had many people by my side, I knew that I alone would have to endure the physical pain that was a part of the recovery. I knew that in spite of my eagerness to get well, there was only one road to recovery, the slow road. And there was no one who could bear this burden for me. The doctors and nurses could use their skills in helping me get back on my feet. My friends and relatives could be of support and encouragement while I was in need. (As an example, my brother had remarked that he wished he could get into the hospital bed in my place for a while and take on my pain in order to give me relief.) But in spite of their help and concern, I knew that I alone would actually *do* the recovering. This gave me a feeling of isolation, as though I were on my own island separated from the real world.

There were many times during my recuperation, usually at night, when I would simply lie back and reflect on what had happened to me. I would specifically recall the intense fear that had come over me in the few split seconds of helplessness just prior to having the accident. I would recall the brief segment in time when I realized that I was about to be involved in a calamity, knowing that it was coming too fast for me to react physically. As I thought back on this brief segment in time, I realized that I had experienced a type of fear never before known to me. For, you see, I did not have a fear of being hurt or bruised, though I knew that was imminent. Rather, my fear was a fear of possible death. To date, this is the most profound emotional experience I have ever had.

As I spent those many days and nights in the hospital, my mind kept going back to the fear of death that had overwhelmed me at the moment of the accident. It seemed wrong to me that my first emotional reaction would be a fear of death (actually fear of God). For most of my life I had been taught that a Christian need not fear death. For most of my life I had felt very secure about my salvation and my relationship with God. Acceptance by the Lord was something I had rarely questioned. But in those silent moments of reflection, I was forced to face the insecure side of my personality.

I became acutely aware that deep down inside there was a firm and uncomfortable recognition of personal and spiritual weaknesses. I was painfully aware that if I were left with my track record, I would be deemed unworthy to enter the kingdom of God. I knew what my weaknesses were, and they were many. And I knew that in spite of my best efforts, many inadequacies would remain. In light of these admissions of weakness, I began to understand my fear at the time of the accident. My deepest emotions had told me that, on my own, I was unworthy to face God and seek His mercy.

These thoughts, centering on my weaknesses and inadequacies, were the actual roots of my feelings of loneliness. I knew that by my sinful nature I had separated myself from God. This is the ultimate loneliness. The irony of the situation was that my lonely feelings were totally unnecessary. For, you see, these feelings were founded upon fear—inappropriate fear. Emotions often play tricks on our minds. Being caught up in the emotion of the moment can cause us to lose sight of some of the most fundamental truths of life. That's what happened to me!

When I was swallowed up by my fear, I assumed that God would not accept me. What a terrible thought! Certainly if I had actually lost God's love and acceptance, I would have had every reason to feel lonely. But the truth is that God never stopped loving me for a moment. My emotions had blinded me to this truth even though it was a fact I had known well for years. I needed to give myself a good dose of realistic thinking in order to bring my unnecessary agitated state to an end.

All of us have slipped into times of loneliness that could have been avoided if we had kept our minds on some basic, fundamental truths. It is easy to become sidetracked by the emotions of the moment. We too readily lose sight of certain facts that can be helpful in those times when our emotions become overwhelming. Unfortunately, many of us become so steeped in our lonely feelings that there seems to be no way out.

There *is* a way out. There *are* appropriate ways of handling loneliness. It would be naive for us to believe that we can live the rest of our lives without ever having another lonely moment if only we stay with a particular "game plan." As long as we live, we will have difficult emotions to deal with. But we can learn to understand and confront our loneliness to the extent that it will not control us or keep us from having a very satisfactory life.

THREE

A PERSONAL EVALUATION

THERE ARE MANY SYMPTOMS of loneliness. Some are obvious, and some are disguised. In general, loneliness can be described as a state of feeling that one does not belong or is not accepted. It could imply intense emotional pain, an empty feeling, a yearning to be with someone, or a restlessness.

We have found the following inventory to be useful in determination of how lonely an individual is. Complete it as quickly as you can! Your first response is usually your most honest answer.

Loneliness Inventory

	TRUE	FALSE
1. I frequently do not feel accepted by a group I am with.	T	F
2. At times I feel as though I do not belong to the group I am with.	T	F
3. At times I have a feeling of inner emotional pain and loneliness.	T	F
4. I often have an empty feeling inside.	T	F
5. I sometimes find myself yearning to be with someone.	T	F
6. It is not unusual for me to have a restless feeling inside.	T	F
7. I frequently worry that others may not accept me.	T	F
8. I have periods in which I feel that others do not want to be around me.	T	F
9. I sometimes feel that others are more intelligent than I am.	T	F
10. I sometimes feel that others are better-looking than I am.	T	F
11. I sometimes feel that others are more socially skilled than I am.	T	F
12. I sometimes feel that others are just more confident in general than I am.	T	F
13. I belong to few organizations.	T	F
14. Even though I belong to several organizations, I do not really feel a part of any of them.	T	F

15. Although I believe in God, at times I do not feel that He is close and near to me. T F
16. My friends often think that I have no problems and that I am always happy, even though on the inside I know better. T F
17. I would like others to see me as rarely being lonely. T F
18. I spend a lot of hours alone. T F
19. I feel that one can never really be close to another individual. T F
20. I seldom associate with people my own age. T F
21. I feel that being a leader is a lonely position. T F
22. At times I find it difficult to trust others. T F
23. I have used alcohol or drugs to escape a lonely feeling inside. T F
24. When I feel lonely, I find myself working very hard. T F
25. I have felt lonely all my life. T F
26. My relationships with others have often been stormy and unstable. T F
27. I sometimes feel rejected even by my closest friends. T F
28. Frequently I withdraw into daydreaming. T F
29. At times I enjoy my own inner fantasy world more than being with people. T F

30. I tend either to overvalue or undervalue the friendship of people around me. T F
31. I like to talk about abstract theories and carry on intellectual conversations, but rarely do I feel really close to people. T F
32. Sometimes I use humor to avoid facing my own loneliness or letting others know how lonely I feel. T F
33. I have many bodily aches and pains. T F
34. At times I wish I had more friends. T F
35. I find myself wishing that I could be more open about my emotional hurts and pains. T F
36. I rarely tell others how I feel when they have hurt me; rather, I tend to withdraw. T F
37. When I feel lonely, I sometimes find myself doing things I know I should not do. T F
38. At times I will not admit to myself how lonely I really feel. T F
39. At times I seem to have an unusual amount of guilt over minor things. T F
40. I often feel angry or sad. T F
41. It seems that I am often helping others, but rarely do others help me. T F
42. I often feel put down by others. T F
43. I have felt so lonely at times that I saw little reason to live. T F
44. I wish I were more popular. T F
45. In high school I was not very popular. T F

46. I participated in few social activities in high school.	T	F
47. I have not dated much.	T	F
48. Others seldom come to see me or call me.	T	F
49. I have often felt inferior to others.	T	F
50. I often find myself preoccupied with my looks.	T	F
51. I often find myself preoccupied with my strivings for success.	T	F
52. Criticism bothers me a great deal.	T	F
53. I often criticize others.	T	F
54. Others have accused me of being aloof.	T	F
55. I seem to lack the ability to form lasting personal relationships.	T	F
56. I am overly sensitive to rejection.	T	F
57. I am somewhat socially withdrawn.	T	F
58. I desire acceptance by others but fear rejection.	T	F
59. I do not desire to be around other people most of the time.	T	F
60. I would enjoy being alone on a one-month vacation at a mountain retreat.	T	F
61. I often worry about my relationships with others.	T	F
62. When I am with others, I develop anxiety symptoms to the point that I feel uncomfortable.	T	F
63. I have never been really intimate with anyone.	T	F
64. I have fewer than a half dozen close friends.	T	F

65. I do not have a sense of being supported by my family or encouraged by the members of my church. T F

Now go back and count the number of "T's" you circled. A score of 20 or less reflects an individual who is not lonely very often. A score of 21 to 29 is average. A score of 30 or more reflects a definite tendency toward loneliness. The rest of this book will be of special benefit to you.

Personality Type and Loneliness

It might seem reasonable to assume that loneliness afflicts some personality types more than others. As a matter of fact, however, the symptoms of loneliness can be experienced by every major personality type.

The Obsessive-Compulsive Personality

The individual with obsessive-compulsive personality traits is perfectionistic and stubborn, tends to become a workaholic, does not readily express warmth, and has underlying insecurities. He is neat, clean, orderly, and dutiful. He is concerned, conscientious, and meticulous (sometimes overly so). He often works so hard that he finds it difficult to relax. Many obsessive-compulsives are very intellectual; in fact, they use their intellect to avoid emotions. They are interested more in facts than in feelings. While they may seem cold to some, to others they seem stable (at least on the surface).

The obsessive-compulsive is often pulled between opposite traits. For example, there may be an inner pull between obedience and defiance. He is usually obedient but occasionally he will be defiant with others. However, this defiance in turn produces a fear that leads him back into his perfectionistic, obedient traits. Another example of being pulled between opposites is that at times the obsessive-compulsive can be very conscientious but at other times negligent. At times he can be very orderly but at other times untidy.

Three main preoccupations are dirt, time, and money. The obsessive-compulsive is usually very clean, very punctual (although some perfectionists are consistently a few minutes late), and very concerned with money (perhaps to the point of being excessively frugal). He may be a very competitive individual. Living for a tomorrow that never comes, he postpones fun and fellowship. Fear stands in the way of his desire to be dependent on others, so he makes an effort to seem very independent. On the surface, then, he appears strong, decisive, and affirmative, but underneath he is uncertain and uneasy and has rigid rules in order to attempt to control his emotions. He has a need to appear perfect. He also has a very strong need for everybody to like him. In fact, he feels that he must *earn* even God's love and acceptance. The reason for this is that, as he grew up, his parents gave the impression that they would accept him only on the condition that he meet their very high expectations. He thinks superhuman achievements will help him to overcome the uncertainties he feels in his world, but he never quite manages to accomplish such achievements.

As is implied by the description above, this individual may suffer from intense loneliness. While he appears strong on the outside, he feels weak on the inside. While he appears to need very little from others, on the inside he feels lonely and wishes to depend on others. His need to win acceptance is an indication that he feels lonely. He never is sure he has done enough for others to accept him. One achievement becomes only a launching pad for another in his effort to be accepted and not left feeling lonely.

The perfectionistic obsessive-compulsive usually chooses a career that requires hard work, long hours, and an environment that discourages intimacy (e.g., dentistry, engineering, computer programming). His attempt to find security by working hard and making a good deal of money does not fill the real insecurity on the inside, which again is related to loneliness. Though he has a good mind, his inner emotions and feelings of loneliness remain. He cannot intellectualize away the lonely feeling he has inside. Theories are no substitutes for friendships. The obsessive-compulsive does keep his emotions a secret from others, but only at the expense of the gnawing pain of resulting loneliness. Fearing rejection not only from others in the family of God but even from God Himself, he goes to all lengths to control his emotions, but the emotion of loneliness will not be controlled. He uses his aloofness and expressions of anger to keep others at a distance, for he fears the closeness that he so desperately desires.

The Histrionic Personality

The individual with histrionic personality traits is usually very different from the perfectionist, although both sets of personality traits can merge in the same individual. The obsessive-compulsive and hysterical personalities do share some common characteristics, one of which is a deep inner feeling of loneliness.

In contrast to the obsessive-compulsive individual, the individual with predominantly histrionic personality traits is likable and outgoing, the life of the party. These individuals are usually dramatic and theatrical, emotional and excitable. On the surface, histrionic (hysterical) males and females seem warm and open. They may be charming and vivacious, but underneath they are immature. Their language may be expressive and they may use many superlatives, exaggerating to dramatize their viewpoints. There may be an aura of egocentricity about them. They are able to put others at ease, though they themselves might not feel at ease. These traits are common among those who choose performing occupations (e.g., salesmen, actors, musicians, pastors, evangelists).

Histrionic personalities may be manipulative, attention-seeking, and seductive in dress and actions. A series of love affairs is common. A female who is primarily histrionic tends to be impressed with older males. An ambivalence toward her father, which is displaced to men in general, may result in her marrying a father-substitute.

Whereas the obsessive-compulsive individual is very time conscious, the histrionic individual could not care less. Whereas the obsessive-compulsive individual's fantasies center around power, the histrionic's fantasies center around receiving love and attention. The histrionic's conversations about theology stress emotional experiences, whereas the obsessive-compulsive stresses abstract intellectual theories. Whereas the obsessive-compulsive individual is extremely disciplined, the histrionic tends to be overly impulsive.

The above description seems to suggest that histrionic individuals would probably never be lonely. But while they are outgoing and friendly on the surface, on the inside they feel lonely. While they are able to put others at ease, they feel ill at ease themselves. While they seem outwardly warm and open, and others think it is easy to get to know them, a deeper intimacy seldom develops. Whereas their dress and actions may be seductive in an attempt to become close to others, the physical closeness does not substitute for the deep inner closeness that they so desire. While they seek members of the opposite sex to be close to physically, they rarely feel close to them emotionally. They may spend much time working on their outward appearance in hopes of receiving attention and acceptance, but on the inside they never really feel accepted or loved. These individuals have trouble developing genuine feelings of love and intimacy. It is as if they are constantly seeking, but never finding, love and attention. Although they give an outward impression of poise and self-confidence, their self-image is one of insecurity, apprehension, and loneliness. Boredom is a persistent problem for these individuals because of their constant loneliness.

Although histrionic individuals are emotional, these are but surface emotions to defend against deep emotions such as loneliness. Their loneliness often goes back to a disturbance at a very young age in their relationship with their parents. In many cases they never felt close to their father so have searched for something to fill that void. Males with histrionic traits may even develop homosexual tendencies because of their yearning to be accepted by their father. They are, of course, confusing sex with emotional intimacy.

The Paranoid Personality

The individual with paranoid personality traits is also prone to loneliness. This individual is characterized by hypersensitivity—he may easily feel slighted. He tends to look for evil motives in others and to expect the worst in every situation. As a result he is overly vigilant and guarded. He may be critical and negative, cynical and skeptical. He may be characterized by several prejudices and a refusal to accept blame. He may seem to be unemotional, cold, and objective, and to lack tenderness, humanness, or softness. There may be a preoccupation with justice or fairness. Prone to jealousy, he may suspect his spouse of infidelity. He may appear hostile and angry.

With respect to theological matters, the individual with paranoid personality traits feels that anyone who disagrees with him is wrong. He may seem tense, anxious, and unsure of himself. He is certainly distrustful and suspicious of others. He views others as unreliable, questions their loyalty, and fears they will treat him unfairly. His behavior is often secretive and seclusive. Since paranoid individuals crave power, many become business executives, politicians, domineering (and nagging) wives, or church leaders. Unfortunately some religious institutions and universities have even taken on the traits of their paranoid leaders.

Given the above personality traits, it is obvious that the paranoid individual will feel lonely. His suspiciousness of others causes him to remain aloof and feel lonely. His hypersensitivity leaves him feeling rejected and mistreated and results in further intensification of his loneliness. His ascribing evil motives to others widens the distance between him and them. Negative and critical thinking causes further isolation. He feels he is a loner—the world's most unusual individual—and, to some extent, he is.

Since the paranoid individual feels ill at ease in social situations, he avoids them and his loneliness mounts. There are various other factors that reinforce the barriers to intimacy with others: his feelings of rejection, his unwillingness to forgive, his intense fear of betrayal, his narcissistic preoccupation with himself, his quarrelsome and argumentative nature, his secretive and seclusive behavior. Many of these traits result from his feeling unloved, but his behavior further alienates people. His aloofness and lack of tenderness and warmth also keep others at a distance from him. His concern with justice and fairness is understandable, but he carries it to an extreme degree, ignoring other equally important issues such as grace and kindness, issues that would encourage closeness.

Deep within, the paranoid individual has an intense longing to be loved by and close to others. But he has a low self-image and feels isolated and alone. His defense against his low self-image and feeling of isolation is his paranoia, which intensifies rather than relieves his loneliness. Theologically, he misinterprets the biblical principle of separation from unbelievers to mean separation from anyone who disagrees with his narrow views; he also deemphasizes the biblical teachings on love.

The Passive-Dependent Personality

The individual with passive-dependent (also called passive-aggressive) personality traits also suffers from loneliness. A basic characteristic of this individual is inadequate performance. No matter what the task, he simply does not do a good job. He may be intentionally (or semi-intentionally) inefficient, forgetful, or just passive in general. He tends to procrastinate and to be consistently late for every appointment and meeting. His dependency traits encourage him to allow others to assume responsibility and give direction. Appearing to be helpless and indecisive, he childishly clings to others in hopes that they will take care of him. But he will not say in a direct manner what he needs or wants; rather, he feels angry and pouts when others do not perceive his needs. Once others do take control, he passively goes along, though at times only halfheartedly. This might be manifested in stubbornness, lack of cooperation, criticism of authority, complaints of being unfairly treated, or attempts to find loopholes. He may find ways to obey the letter rather than the spirit of the law.

The passive-dependent personality has a low self-image. In many cases he is the youngest child of a domineering parent. A basic problem is an anger he feels he dare not express. In general he is immature: witness his childish desire for others to tell him what to do. He wants to receive more than to give. With respect to religious matters, he probably exhibits the halfhearted compliance characteristic of many church members today. He is attracted to churches or organizations with a strong leader to dominate and think for him. Many passive-dependent individuals are attracted to the armed services as a career for the same reasons. Some become dependent on drugs or alcohol to kill their pains of loneliness. They are lonely primarily because they are too passive and emotionally lazy to *do* what it takes to build rewarding, long-term, intimate relationships.

The passive-dependent individual's behavior is self-defeating. His unwillingness to be alone and overdependence on others accomplish exactly the opposite of what he hopes. They serve to alienate and drive others from him. In addition, his refusal to tell others his needs in a straightforward, healthy manner results in their responding incorrectly to his needs. All of these factors intensify a basic loneliness that is already present.

The Sociopathic Personality

The sociopathic personality also suffers form loneliness. He is basically selfish, callous, irresponsible, and impulsive. He has no feelings of guilt and does not learn from experience. As a consequence, there is often a record of repeated conflicts with society. The first of these conflicts nearly always occurred at home with his parents, whom he manipulated into spoiling him. The school history is often one of poor performance and frequent absenteeism. Likewise, the work history is one of irresponsibility and frequent job changes. There is often a history of legal and social offenses as well—lying, stealing, cheating, blaming others, drug or alcohol abuse, homosexuality or promiscuity.

Sociopathic individuals live by the pleasure principle; they cannot tolerate frustration and have difficulty deferring pleasure. In other words, they do whatever they want whenever they want—with total disregard for others. There is a history of not being loyal to either social values or any other person. They are often manipulative and sadistic. Although there may be an air of self-assurance and a superficial likability about them, their lack of warmth and tenderness results in a lack of closeness to others. They may hold to a form of religion, but this is hypocritical. They try to boss God around, expecting Him to fulfill their every whim and desire.

Indeed, the sociopathic individual lives a lonely life. Lacking a sense of personal identity, he has felt misunderstood from childhood. While he is likable on the surface and able to make a great first impression, no depth nor intimacy ever develops. Anyone who tries to get close to him is doomed to disappointment because he regards people as only objects to be used, merely characters that come and go in his life. Interpersonal relationships are exploited and would-be friends are driven away. He may seek stimulation to fill the inner emptiness and loneliness, but the stimulation is never enough. Since he does not learn from experience and therefore has repeated conflicts with society, he ends up feeling even more isolated, persecuted, and alone.

The Schizoid Personality

The individual with schizoid personality traits appears to be the most lonely of all. He (or she) is characterized by shyness, seclusiveness, an avoidance of close relationships, and a withdrawal into his own inner world. He has a reputation for being an aloof and eccentric loner. Socially repressed and isolated, he is afraid and suspicious of others, fearful that they may be talking about him. He may even seem to be indifferent to their praise.

The schizoid individual has probably been lonely all his life. Raised in a home in which there was little display of affection, he may have tried, at the age of two or three, to get close to his parents but felt rejected and withdrew. With a low self-image, he feels inadequate and unimportant and has an intense sensitivity to rejection by others. He has great difficulty in forming relationships; in fact, he simply does not form relationships.

His obvious need for privacy, his secretive behavior, and his lack of facial expression discourage others from attempting to draw near to him.

The Cyclothymic Personality

Individuals with cyclothymic personality traits are characterized by alternating periods of elation and depression. After a period of elation (or a very high mood), which may last for days, weeks, or even months, there follows a period of normality, which is in turn followed by a period of depression. When these individuals are in their high mood, they may seem ambitious, warm, enthusiastic, and optimistic; they may exhibit a high level of energy, accelerated speech, and increased motor activity, as well as a decreased need for sleep. During these euphoric stages they are often very likable and have a contagious sense of humor, although there may be an edge of hostility and sarcasm to it. They may lack sensitivity toward others in these hypomanic episodes. They may be more irritable and their judgment may become somewhat impaired. In these episodes they may be impulsive, and they may make commitments they cannot fulfill. Although they may seem effervescent and cheerful, in reality these periods of euphoria may be only a defense against feelings of depression and loneliness.

Often these periods of euphoria are followed by a period of feeling extremely blue, sad, and lonely. During the depressed episodes the individual may feel hopeless and helpless and have extreme guilt about both major and minor offenses in his past. During a hypomanic episode the individual may be grandiose and avoid any self-criticism. However, during the depressive phase, he has a very low self-image and is extremely critical of himself. In the hypomanic episode he may exploit the vulnerability of others, but during the depressive episode he sees only his own faults and runs himself down. During the hypomanic episode he tends to refuse to acknowledge any problems he might have or loneliness he might feel, whereas during the depressive phase these are overwhelming.

The Dysthymic Personality

The dysthymic individual has a history of many years of depression. This individual may look sad and indeed feels very sad, hopeless, and helpless. Characterized by painful thinking and a low self-image, he is introspective in a self-derogatory way. He feels guilty about many things, not only major events but also minor events of his past. He continually worries over past mistakes and sins.

The dysthymic person feels isolated. He has a tremendous need to depend on others, and yet he fears rejection or expects others to disappoint him and not meet his needs. In fact, however, he usually sets himself up for rejection and then concludes that he can really trust no one—that in the end everyone will reject him. He is indeed a lonely individual. His loneliness may reach such proportions that he can no longer sleep at night. Although he yearns to be close to others and find release from the emotional pain he feels, this individual may be characterized by an irritability that drives others away and further complicates his own loneliness. The end point of his emotional pain is thoughts of suicide. He begins to believe that anything, even death, would be better than the painful thinking that he is experiencing and the emotional isolation that he feels.

The Depressed Personality

Many depressed individuals come from homes in which the parents were depressed. Or they may come from homes in which a parent was absent almost all of the time (or essentially absent because of his work schedule). Also, the parents may have been harsh, leaving the child with the feeling that he was no good and deserved to be alone. Or the parents may have been rejecting. In any event, the result was the same. The child developed feelings of depression and inner loneliness.

The Narcissistic Personality

The narcissistic personality has feelings of grandiose self-importance and is preoccupied with his own success. In Greek mythology Narcissus was a youth who fell in love with himself upon seeing his own reflection in a pond. He became so preoccupied with his own reflection that he would not leave. Similarly, the narcissistic individual is extremely caught up in himself and his own success. At the same time he is an extremely lonely individual with a lifelong history of trouble in his relationships with others. He tends to exploit others, to feel that he is entitled to use them, and to have little empathy for them. His focusing solely on himself is a very lonely position. Lack of intimacy prevents any kind of personal growth.

The Borderline Personality

The borderline personality disorder is characterized by extreme swings of mood, by impulsivity, by uncertainty with respect to self-image, and by instability in interpersonal relationships. We recall one individual who had all of these symptoms. At times he would become very angry for little apparent reason. His interpersonal relationships were unstable. But what impressed us most was his intense feeling of loneliness. He would call us often, in effect begging for help with his feeling of being alone. Friends had attempted to help him, but still the chronic loneliness had remained. His clinging dependency drove people away until he learned in therapy to overcome his faulty behavior patterns.

The Healthy Personality

After studying the traits of the various personalities described above, the reader may question whether any individual is healthy. The fact is that all individuals have, to some degree, traits of each type of personality. In most cases these traits tend to balance out one another. Only when a trait goes to an extreme degree does it become an overt disorder.

Another question the reader might have is whether the healthy individual ever experiences loneliness. The answer is that the healthy individual does feel lonely at times. This is only normal and human. However, he continues to function well and the episode is only transient and brief. The healthy individual has a strength from within so that the loneliness does not overwhelm him. He is able to keep his sense of humor. He is able to deal not only with surface feelings but also with deep feelings and to admit his faults and problems, including loneliness.

The healthy individual will have developed a support system of friends, so that during times of loneliness he may draw from them. He is able to be open and honest with others. He is intimate with others and willing to give to them rather than only to receive from them. Although at times he does have conflicts with others, he continues to trust them and is always willing to forgive them.

Thus, although everyone feels lonely at times, the healthy individual is still able to function well. The episodes are usually transient and brief because, when feelings of loneliness do come, he has an arsenal of means—especially a support system of friends and a walk with God—to help him cope.

PART 2

THE CAUSES AND CONSEQUENCES OF LONELINESS

FOUR

THE RIVER RUNS DEEP

The Pervasiveness of Loneliness

LONELINESS IS AN EXPERIENCE common to millions of Americans. In order to counteract loneliness many have turned to singles' bars, encounter groups, drugs, free sex, and the Eastern religions that are so popular today.

The noted Swiss psychiatrist Paul Tournier tells the story of a lonely lady who would turn on her radio in the evening just to hear the announcer say in a friendly voice, "We bid you a very pleasant good night!" She was so lonely that even an impersonal voice was a comfort to her.

We were sharing this story with one of our group therapy sessions, and at the end of the story we commented, "Of course, none of us are that lonely." Then all of a sudden an elderly lady interrupted us and said, "Why, I am." We should not have been surprised, for every week we counsel people who, in their own way, say, "I am so lonely; I feel no one really cares for me. If only someone cared!"

In a recent survey 26 percent of those polled indicated they had felt very lonely at some point during the preceding few weeks. In 1967 Thomas Holmes published "The Stress of Adjusting to Change," a study of the amount of stress caused by various situations. It is noteworthy that loneliness is somehow involved in what were discovered to be the five most stressful situations—the death of a spouse, divorce, marital separation, a jail term, and the death of a close family member other than a spouse. A majority of those seeking psychiatric help feel very lonely. Loneliness is a problem especially for the elderly, often resulting in suicide. However, loneliness strikes all ages and all classes.

Although loneliness is pervasive in our culture, until relatively recently very little was written on it. For some reason (probably a search for some meaning to life that would deal with the increasing inner loneliness of people), it has become a popular subject during the past few years for both secular and Christian authors. Now imagine, if you will, that you are a lonely soul desperately in need of help; you are holding on to life with only a thread of hope. Suppose also that you run across a book on loneliness by a well-known secular psychologist. You think that at last there may be some hope. So what if my parents didn't want me, my wife left me, and even the dog leaves the room when I enter? Perhaps this book offers some real help. Eagerly your eyes race to the back cover where you read, "Everyone needs to experience the pain of loneliness to become reacquainted with himself—to know the glory of being himself and setting up an honest, personal value system. Being lonely is a desolate, critical state—but, being lonely can bring you in touch with yourself." You conclude that there really is no hope, for, unlike the well-known psychologist, you do not believe that there is anything to be gained from the desolate, critical state of loneliness.

You are just about to give up when you spot a magazine containing an article on overcoming loneliness. You quickly flip through the pages. Then your eyes fall on the following advice: "One sure way to kick the everyday blues is to start to trust the instinct that tells you to 'get up and get moving.' Take action that will change your state of mind or your physical surroundings . . . get involved with something you enjoy . . . because when you're doing something you like, you're never lonely, even though you may be doing it alone."

You think, "Not bad advice," so you double your activities. You join the health club and build a he-man physique. You join the local Jaycees and take part in other community activities; you become active in politics, but to your amazement your problem remains—you still feel lonely.

Don't give up yet. There is hope. . . .

Much has been written regarding the causes of and cures for loneliness. Certainly, the magazine was not entirely wrong in suggesting that loneliness is caused by inactivity. Nor was the psychologist totally off base in stating that when we fail to accept our emotions, our chances for overcoming them are lessened. Yet, as we will discover in the next few pages, the roots of loneliness run much deeper than the psychologist and the magazine suggest.

Surely the best source for discovering the causes of and cures for loneliness is the Bible. The word *alone* or its equivalent is found more than a hundred times in the Bible, but in the majority of cases it does not imply a state of loneliness. Being alone and being lonely are not necessarily the same. One can be alone but not lonely.

Among those infrequent instances in which the Bible implies a state of being lonely are 1 Kings 19 (Elijah) and 2 Timothy 4:9–10 (Paul). David uses the word *lonely* in Psalm 25:16–18 (NASB):

> Turn to me and be gracious to me,
> For I am lonely and afflicted.
> The troubles of my heart are enlarged;
> Bring me out of my distresses.
> Look upon my affliction and my trouble,
> And forgive all my sins.

The Causes of Loneliness

Before proceeding we should define *loneliness*. Loneliness is a state of feeling that one is not accepted or does not belong. It implies varying degrees of emotional pain, an empty feeling, a yearning to be with someone, a restlessness. From our study of the Bible and experience as psychiatrists we have concluded that there are five general causes of loneliness.

1. Isolation from God

It has been said that there is a God-vacuum in each of us. People may deny it; they may fight it. But they cannot fill the lonely void that only Jesus Christ can fill.

Of course, even Christians experience to some degree this isolation from God as a result of breaking fellowship with Him by sin. Adam and Eve experienced that loneliness. David experienced that loneliness. We talk with Christians weekly who are experiencing that loneliness because sin has broken their fellowship with God, their heavenly Father.

2. Our Changing Society

We live in a society that tends to promote loneliness. Our society is fast, mobile, and changing. Every year 20 percent of the families in America move. On Manhattan, one can come in contact with hundreds of thousands of people in a very brief time span. Although we may come in contact with thousands, there is not enough time to build relationships, and so people are lonely.

Also, because of television there is much less time for personal communication. Even what little time people have for each other in our mobile society is often spent in loneliness in front of a television set. Research shows that excessive television watching also causes individuals to trust others less and thus promotes even more loneliness. Our changing society also has produced a new set of values, such as excessive individualism and independence, that encourages loneliness.

3. Rejecting Others

In our psychiatric practice we commonly see individuals who are lonely because they have rejected others. They have fallen victim to a situation they set up themselves. For various reasons (such as their own pride, inferiority complex, or shyness) they have rejected others. In his best-selling book *Why Am I Afraid to Tell You Who I Am?*, John Powell points out that many individuals are afraid to be open with others for fear that if they are open they will be rejected. Thus, in order to avoid rejection, an individual may reject others before they have a chance to reject him. What it boils down to is that individuals frequently reject others because they do not like or accept themselves.

4. Being Rejected by Others

There are some who are lonely because they have been rejected by others. Perhaps they have a critical spirit and others do not want to be around them. Perhaps they are the victim of circumstances; for example, a wife who is neglected by a busy husband. Perhaps it may not be their fault at all; for example, the Christian who is rejected by his non-Christian friends because of his Christian values.

5. Neglect in Childhood

It is amazing how our society has failed in its responsibilities to its children. In our culture people divorce and fathers are too busy for their children. The results are devastating. We spent time recently with an adolescent who had tried to kill himself. As we talked with him he seemed ecstatic to have our attention for a brief period of time. He had been desperately lonely because his father was never home.

We have reviewed briefly five general causes of loneliness. The river of loneliness truly runs deep today. In chapters 5 and 6, we will examine in greater detail some specific causes of loneliness.

FIVE

ME AGAINST THE WORLD

THIS CHAPTER EXPLORES some of the specific causes of loneliness. They range in scope all the way from world society in general to the nuclear family.

Our Changing Technological Society

Have you ever noticed how our highly technical society tends to alienate people from one another? Have you ever been bothered by the fact that with our many sophisticated capabilities the individual seems to take a back seat to computers? Our world seems to be controlled by machines. For example, whenever you have questions regarding your bill from the local department store or the telephone company, you have to wait to find out what the computer has to say. Even when you go to the small ice-cream shop, your hopes for a little personal contact with the salesperson are dashed when you have to take a number to be waited on. This causes a sense of depersonalization in our interactions with fellow human beings. How many times in dealing with a gas station attendant or a secretary have you felt you were being treated like a nobody? Too many times, no doubt.

While it is amazing to see how scientists have been able to make astounding practical use of their knowledge, it is sad to witness the sometimes dehumanizing effect it has on individuals. This can result in a "me-against-the-world" feeling. As a simple example, you have probably seen some poor soul kicking away at a vending machine that has swallowed his coins. There are times when we feel like the lone warrior at battle against the mighty army called Technology. During these times we feel genuinely isolated.

The World Situation

In addition to the difficulties caused by technological advance we are living in an age of political and economic instability. Social unrest causes personal tensions to rise. The word *crisis* seems to be one of the most overused words in the news media. Yet, realistically, we recognize that crisis situations are indeed multiplying. We have crises involving international affairs, energy, inflation, and unemployment. The list could go on and on. Simply watching the evening news on television can be discouraging because the bad news virtually always outweighs the good news.

Do you remember watching with horror and rage the reports of the Iranian takeover of the United States embassy in Tehran? We all shared a common sense of helplessness. How about when the local news reports that burglaries, murders, and rapes are on the increase? Again, there is this same feeling of helplessness. Why, it's even irritating to think that you have to lock the door every time you get into your car or whenever you leave your car to go into a store.

Such an atmosphere of tenseness and turmoil takes its toll on the individual. You are, no doubt, familiar with the empty feeling that can come in the face of such complex problems. It is not uncommon for a person to feel like an innocent bystander who can only grit his teeth as he watches these events pass by. We grudgingly feel as though we have no choice but to accept the burdens that come as a result of events that are out of our control.

Consequently, many people feel like a small, insignificant drop of water being tossed about in a sea of turbulence. We recognize that even large social and political bodies are often unsuccessful in dealing with crisis situations. And by comparison an individual seems pitifully powerless. It is obvious that a feeling of impotence and loneliness can engulf an individual who feels overwhelmed by such grave social conditions.

Breakdown of the Nuclear Family

Tremendous changes are occurring in the traditional family setting. In recent years the number of divorces has escalated. Live-in arrangements between men and women are becoming a more commonly accepted alternative to marriage. Child-custody cases are causing children to feel torn in their loyalties toward their parents. It is an exception to the rule to find families who actually enjoy a spirit of unity.

To make matters worse, it is amazing how our culture has failed in its responsibility to our youth. Television shows and movies make no apologies for the way they try to lure young people's attention toward immoral programming. Even commercials proudly display teenagers as the up-and-coming sex idols. So much revolves around teaching young people to be sexy. It's frightening to think that powerful figures in the entertainment world have seemingly no regard for the effects their work has on the family structure. They are subtly teaching (often not so subtly) that the sanctity of marriage and the family is something of the past. They teach living for the present moment, with relatively no regard for the future. These people do not realize (or care) that they are leading masses of young people into a lifestyle that will guarantee loneliness.

Because of all this, people are questioning the traditional thought that marriage and family living offer a unique opportunity for rewarding interpersonal relationships. Many have felt like losers in their attempts to sustain satisfying relationships. So rather than continuing their positive efforts, they give up and begin grasping at anything that offers even temporary pleasure. It seems that failure breeds failure. When the youth of today witness the failure of traditional family arrangements, they often become pessimistic with respect to their own plans for the future.

We have often heard adolescents talk bitterly about how they do not want to be responsible for bringing children into such a "messed-up" world. Family breakups have taken a heavy toll on their sense of self-esteem and feelings of belongingness. Many are lonely because key family members are not at home. They find they have no one with whom they can share themselves emotionally. There seems to be a genuine increase in frustration among both youth and adults who seem hungry for someone's attention. Family turbulence and breakdowns certainly can result in feelings of despair and discouragement.

Childhood Experiences

We have seen that when there is a breakdown of the traditional family, those involved will experience some loneliness. But even in some traditional families there can be patterns of interaction that cause a sense of loneliness.

The way you were brought up as a child is usually the greatest influence on the way you behave years later as an adult. It can be helpful to examine your past in an effort to understand how your present patterns of living originated. Of course, the intention of examining some of the events in your childhood is not that you learn to blame Mom or Dad for your way of life. They were bringing you up in the best way they knew how.

The remainder of this chapter will examine several patterns that, established in a person's early years, may make it easy to slip into a mood of loneliness.

Emotional Dependence

It is frequently found that people who feel lonely as an adult had a reasonably comfortable childhood because Mom and Dad would do many things for them above and beyond the call of duty. Mom and Dad may have been so helpful and accommodating that the child seemingly had everything he needed. Whenever the child needed anything, there was no doubt that one of the parents would be there to take care of the matter. However, this type of "you-can-count-on-me" approach often goes too far. Sometimes parents are so overprotective and accommodating toward their children that the children do not learn appropriate personal responsibilities. As these children grow up, they tend to try to re-create the same safe, protective atmosphere. The problem is that this often is not realistic. The world will not spoil them as their parents did, nor should it. This would only be promoting the irresponsibility taught in early childhood.

Here is an illustration: Becky was a twenty-year-old who had lived in a small town all of her life but had just recently moved to take a job in a big city two hundred miles away from home. Upon moving to the city, she found herself feeling quite lonely and depressed. It is natural for someone to have to go through a period of transition when making a move as big as this one. But Becky's lonely feelings would not go away. She was outgoing, so she met many people and had an active social life. Her job was satisfactory. Unable to understand why her lonely feelings continued, she came in for counseling.

In her counseling sessions, Becky revealed that she had had a very pleasant childhood. Her mother was the type of mom the other children wished for. Whenever Becky had friends over, Mom was right there fixing them a feast. Whenever Becky needed money, Mom would give it upon request. Whenever Becky had a problem, she knew that she could go to Mom for the answers she so desperately wanted. When she was old enough to drive, her parents bought her a car; she didn't have to work to pay for it herself. In fact, they gave her the family credit card so she wouldn't have to buy her own gas. At the time, it seemed as though Becky had everything she needed—and more.

Given this background one could have predicted that Becky was not going to be very well equipped for handling her responsibilities as an adult. And that's exactly what happened! Because she never learned to develop the necessary skills to confront difficult situations, she grew up needy. And because no one in her new world could possibly know how to (or would even want to) meet her every need as Mom and Dad once had, she began to feel very lonely. What had apparently been an ideal family life for a young girl eventually backfired when she found herself unable to re-create the same environment as an adult.

Ultra-close Parental Control

We turn now to a family pattern somewhat similar to the one just discussed, with the exception that this pattern is not quite so ideal for the youngster. In cases in which the child is made emotionally dependent, he feels safe and protected. In cases of ultra-close parental control, he feels trapped.

In an effort to be helpful, many parents go overboard in guiding their children. Many children grow up in an environment in which the vast majority of their outside activities are controlled by Mom and Dad. They feel forced into complying with the wishes of their parents, whether they like it or not. These children usually feel that their personal boundaries are being violated, so they develop a strong desire to make independent decisions. These children resent that they have no choice in what happens in their lives. Can you see how this could plant seeds of rebellion?

A young man named Steve came from such a family background. As an adult he grappled constantly with depression; examination of his problem revealed that he was a very lonely person. Steve had grown up in a home in which success was all-important. His father was a tremendous success in the business world. He liked to talk of how he had picked himself up by the bootstraps and made something of his life. Naturally, he expected the same of his son. He wanted his son to study hard and make all A's on his report card. Then he wanted him to attend college and get a master's in business administration or a law degree, or maybe both. Sports was considered important, so Dad pushed his son into football and baseball. Of course, nothing could make him happier than Steve's making a game-winning play or being voted as the most valuable player.

Steve's mother became involved too. She knew that music would help round out her son, so she insisted that he take music lessons. She also wanted him to be a fine Christian, so she forced him to go to every church activity available for young people. Of course, if Steve ever talked back to his parents or expressed a desire different from theirs, he was made to feel guilty.

As Steve looked back upon those years, he realized that his parents often had good intentions, and indeed many of their "suggestions" made good sense. Yet he resented the fact that he rarely, if ever, had any say in what took place in his life. As he remembered it, he was never asked what he was thinking about doing or what he would like to do—he was *told* what he would do. Oh, there were family discussions, all right. But the discussions always seemed to be an explanation as to why he should do what his parents wanted.

When parents continually force themselves on a child against his will, the child will either grow up so passive and dependent that he can't cope (resulting in drug addiction, alcoholism, schizophrenia, etc.), or he will grow up doggedly determined to make his own decisions. In the latter case he will allow no one to tell him what to do. As an adult he will shy away from developing emotional involvement with others for fear of losing his sense of autonomy, as he did as a child. This will result in his turning down legitimate requests from others, which he interprets as demands—his life has been controlled by others long enough; now it is his turn. Unfortunately, this "don't-tell-me-what-to-do" attitude causes individuals to become estranged from others, increasing the likelihood of loneliness.

Feeling Left Out

As we have already discussed, the feeling of being left out is becoming more and more widespread due to an increasingly impersonal world. Unfortunately, this feeling often has its roots in the family system, tending to be strongest in people whose parents or siblings were either emotionally passive or abusive. It often occurs in families in which key members are frequently absent. Many children have grown up feeling starved for some sort of positive (or even negative) emotional attention. When children get little attention, they may automatically assume that they are insignificant or of little value.

Many of them, given their circumstances, will grow up feeling insecure about who they are.

One such example is Norma. Norma's mother usually had very little to say to anyone. An outsider might have been able to determine that Norma's mother had many insecurities, but to Norma she just seemed unconcerned. Norma's parents had divorced when she was five. For most of her childhood, she depended solely on Mom.

Now, Norma would be the first to admit that her mother was quite adequate in providing for her physical needs. She always had food to eat and clothes to wear. Her mother always saw to it that she got off to school on time. But the thing that stuck in Norma's mind was that she and her mother rarely had anything to talk about. Her mother was silent most of the time; it seemed as though she would talk to her daughter only when it was necessary to get something done. Norma imitated this, of course; that is, when she was around her friends, she usually had little to contribute to the conversation. Consequently, she was not very skilled in making friends. To top it off, she hardly ever heard from her father. It seemed to her that he didn't even know she existed. Everywhere she turned there was nothing but emptiness.

People such as Norma grow into adulthood desperately desiring closeness to someone, anyone. One of two patterns is likely to emerge from this type of background. These people may feel so inadequate that they fear opening themselves up to anyone, so a pattern of shyness and withdrawal emerges. Or they might make every possible effort to create closeness through constantly hovering around others, making demands of them, or forcing an artificial togetherness. In either case, persons with this type of background eventually slip into loneliness since neither withdrawal nor forced togetherness is likely to bring satisfaction to life.

Excessive Punishment or Criticism

Children need discipline and constructive criticism as they grow up. Unfortunately, there is an all-too-common belief that discipline and punishment are always one and the same. Consequently, many parents rear their children with a heavy overemphasis on the punishment aspects of parenting. These children get the feeling that it is not acceptable to be imperfect, to make mistakes. Excessive punishment causes them to feel that they are loved and accepted only when they behave correctly.

Larry grew up in a family that everyone would describe as being of the highest moral standard. His parents were well respected by their peers. Quite naturally they tried to teach Larry and his siblings the differences between right and wrong. They gave him instructions as to how to handle himself with other people. They taught him good table manners and social etiquette. And when he did something that did not meet their approval, he was punished. Sounds quite normal, doesn't it?

But Larry recalled that he often felt very uncomfortable, unaccepted, and unappreciated in his childhood. He was deathly afraid of ever making a mistake, because he felt rejected for even minor mistakes. At the same time he knew that he had flaws. His parents had expected so much perfection from him that he was afraid to be himself. From experience, he knew that if he made even an honest mistake, he would be punished for it. In his parents' book, there was no such thing as an honest mistake.

Larry's parents were correct in teaching solid values and morals to him. They were incorrect in taking it to such an extreme that their son felt he was not understood or accepted whenever he did something wrong. In essence, Larry felt as though he was constantly under the threat of being judged bad or wrong.

When people such as Larry realistically recognize that they will always make some mistakes, they begin to cringe at the thought of being told, "You're wrong," or "You're bad." When overdone, such criticisms by parents begin to lose their intended effectiveness. Their children will carry into adulthood a need to be accepted as imperfect. When this need is not met, they may become angry and push others away. Or they may enter adulthood feeling battered down, believing they will never be able to make the grade. They feel defeated. In any case you can see how this type of background can lead to feelings of loneliness.

While the types of family backgrounds we have examined cannot possibly represent the full spectrum, there is at least enough here for you to recognize that in childhood there is a potential to develop patterns that can produce lifelong loneliness. We are creatures of habit and we tend to continue in our adult lives the same patterns that were started in childhood.

However, there is hope. Remember that these life patterns are learned. They were learned at a time in life when the individual was not mentally capable of thinking through all of the ramifications of his or her behavior patterns. As adults, we are more able to examine our lives and make conscious decisions to change the patterns that are not healthy. What was once learned can be unlearned or relearned differently.

Even though there are many outside factors (involving society in general and our families) that contribute to loneliness, much of it is actually self-inflicted. Whenever we allow these outside factors to influence and control us, we are ourselves just as responsible for the lonely feelings within. Many of these outside factors cannot be changed. But the loneliness that is brought on by ourselves can be overcome.

Usually change comes at a time in our lives when we admit to ourselves that we are not pleased with our patterns of responding to life and are open to exploring ways of thinking, feeling, and reacting differently. We do not have to be burdened forever by circumstances that cause loneliness.

We are not yet finished with our discussion of the specific causes of loneliness. There is one major factor that needs to be addressed, as uncomfortable as it may be to face up to—the sin factor. We will examine this factor in chapter 6.

SIX

THE SIN FACTOR—THE ULTIMATE ORIGIN OF LONELINESS

Mankind's Wrong Choice

IN GAINING AN UNDERSTANDING of loneliness, it is helpful to become aware of the social and family factors that serve to create an atmosphere for loneliness. But to say that they are the only causes of loneliness would be incorrect. To gain a complete understanding of loneliness we must look at the ultimate factor—sin.

Originally in the perfectly created world of Adam and Eve there was no such thing as loneliness. Man's creation was the high point in the formation of the world. We are told in Genesis 2:18 that God decided, "It is not good that man should be alone." God's desire for man was that he should never feel lonely. So God created Eve to be Adam's helper, his companion for life. Human relationships were a safeguard given by God to eliminate man's potential for loneliness.

In their original condition, Adam and Eve possessed the perfect ability to fulfill one another's emotional and physical needs. Each felt loved in a most significant way. They each were able to appreciate the euphoric life that God had granted them. Because of God's gracious gift of human companionship, man was able to experience love in a way that kept him from knowing loneliness. And, no doubt, this gift of human relations helped man appreciate and experience the love of God in a most rewarding way.

But everything changed when sin became a part of the human experience. You see, when God created man He gave him a free will. God did not want all of mankind to love Him simply because they were programmed to do so. He wanted man's love for Him to be a choice. Consequently, mankind had the choice to draw close to God or to go their own way. Unfortunately, Adam and Eve decided to go against God in an attempt to make themselves little gods. With the onset of sin they thrust mankind into a lifestyle of self-centeredness. Here is the account of Adam and Eve's choice to go against God's wishes by eating the forbidden fruit:

> When the woman saw that the tree was good for food, and that it was a delight to the eyes, and that the tree was desirable to make one wise, she took from its fruit and ate; and she gave also to her husband with her, and he ate. Then the eyes of both of them were opened, and they knew that they were naked; and they sewed fig leaves together and made themselves loin coverings.

> And they heard the sound of the Lord God walking in the garden in the cool of the day, and the man and his wife hid themselves from the presence of the Lord God among the trees of the garden.
>
> GENESIS 3:6–8 NASB

As you can see from the Genesis account, with the fall of man into sin, Adam and Eve became separated from God and from each other. They brought imperfection upon humanity by their wrong choice. They became incapable of experiencing love and interpersonal relations in their most complete form. At that moment loneliness was born. Its birth came during humanity's darkest hour.

To this day, because of sin everyone knows what loneliness feels like. We each have the option of choosing to follow self or God, and we each at some time have made the wrong choice just as Adam and Eve did. No one is capable of experiencing perfect communion with a fellow human or with God the way Adam and Eve did before sin. We would like to, but our humanness prevents it. In spite of our very best efforts, we all have failures in our relationships with one another and in our relationship with God. This sad reality is a direct result of sin.

Fortunately, this loneliness is not the sum total of our experience. *It is not all-encompassing.* There are times when we are able to step out of this lonely existence and become genuinely connected with God and with other humans. Though loneliness is an inevitable result of sin, out of grace God has kept the lines of relationship open. In later chapters we will explore some of the ways to overcome loneliness. So keep in mind that although loneliness is inevitable because of sin, it does not have to get the best of us.

We are taught that "in everything God works for good with those who love him, who are called according to his purpose" (Rom. 8:28 RSV). Surely this truth can be applied to the problem of loneliness. Though loneliness originates in darkness, it can cause us to move toward the light. The person who steps from a cold, dark cave into bright sunlight greatly appreciates the sun's warmth and the beauty of the world around him. Such can be the case for the person who confronts his loneliness and allows it to open his eyes to the richness and beauty of the light and warmth found in God's world.

Rather than something to be feared or avoided, confronting loneliness can lead to many significant resolutions—resolutions regarding how we will handle our emotions and what our purpose in life will be. It can lead to discovering the real meaning of love, peace, and solitude. There is reassurance in the fact that God's response to the loneliness of humanity is not to back away from us but to become more deeply involved in redeeming us from our human condition. In working through the deep valleys of loneliness we can actually begin to come to grips with the most meaningful facts of existence.

Redefining Loneliness

Now that we have traced the origin of loneliness to the Garden of Eden, let us redefine loneliness: Loneliness is an experience of isolation resulting from an individual's separation from God, separation from others, and displeasure with self. It is accompanied by a lack of inner peace and contentment. There is an uneasy feeling about the way life is going when we feel lonely. Loneliness implies emotional pain, an empty feeling, a yearning to be with someone, a restlessness.

Separation from God

There is a God-vacuum in each of us. There is a hole within ourselves that only a meaningful relationship with God can fill. But when it comes to loneliness, atheists do not have the corner on the market. (In fact, many atheists will deny that they feel lonely because they deny their need for God.) Even dedicated Christians are quite capable of feeling this separation from God as a result of breaking fellowship with Him by sin. We talk with Christians daily who are experiencing a loneliness that is a result of a break in their relationship with God because of sin. Because they are still imperfect, Christians continue to have emotional struggles.

As mentioned earlier, in God's original creation humanity was perfect. Scripture tells us that God created man and He saw that "it was good." Consequently, man was able to enjoy a perfect sense of fellowship with his Creator. He was able to know God in a rich and rewarding way. Perfect communion with God was simply a fact of life.

But man's fall into sin radically changed this relationship. Adam and Eve had the choice to obey God or to disobey Him. They chose to disobey. The moment they committed this first sin they felt ashamed and embarrassed before God. They tried to hide from Him. Having chosen imperfection, they knew that this was impossible. They were so distinctly aware of the wide gulf they had placed between themselves and God that they felt deep shame. But in spite of their sense of guilt and remorse over their wrongdoing, they continued to sin.

As we examine our lives today, we must admit that we too have chosen to allow sin to become a part of our lives. We have carried on the tradition begun by Adam and Eve. Consequently, we too must face the consequences of our choices just as they did. We realize that in our bare human form we are unworthy to assume a perfect union with God. God originally offered a life of perfection, but humans chose a life of separation.

Separation from Others

Let's examine further our illustration of Adam and Eve. When sin entered their lives, they were not only ashamed and embarrassed before God, they were ashamed before one another. They felt a need to cover themselves with fig leaves, representing the fact that they did not feel comfortable in being totally vulnerable. Because deceit had been involved in the fall of man, there entered into their relationship a lack of trust and a lack of openness. Sin drove a wedge between two perfectly created individuals. To this day, there is no one person who knows and understands another person in the most complete and honest way. Like Adam and Eve, we encounter walls in our interactions with one another. Our desire, of course, is to lower these walls, but as long as we are imperfect, they will exist.

It is because of this feeling of separation from others that most people complain of loneliness. In spite of the fact that there is no such thing as a perfect human relationship, many people hold on to the naive notion that somewhere out there is a person who can meet their every emotional need. It is precisely this type of dreaming that can set a person up for severe loneliness and depression. Even when these individuals encounter one disappointment after another, they still hold on to the idealized thought that others ought to be everything they want them to be.

Examine yourself. You will notice that there is a genuine reluctance to reveal your full self to others, for that would place you in a position of vulnerability. You will readily admit that it is often frightening to reveal and share some of the deep secrets of your soul with another person. We are reluctant to reveal anything that will widen the gaps that sin has already placed between ourselves and others.

Sad as it may seem, as long as we are imperfect, we will never be able to become involved in a perfect relationship. We have good intentions, desiring to fill the gaps and tear down the walls between ourselves and others—and there are many who succeed in building satisfying relationships. But though many relationships are solid and healthy, each of us is forced at some point to face the reality that no single relationship can be absolutely complete.

Displeasure with Self

Wouldn't it be nice to be perfect? We all have thoughts and dreams about what our lives would be like if we were able to live without sin. In fact, to some extent, we all formulate goals that are based on such thoughts and dreams. But many of us become disillusioned with ourselves when we realize that we are not perfect. At times, when we fall short of our idealistic thoughts and dreams, we get very angry at ourselves. All of us do this to some extent.

When we are being totally honest with ourselves, we sadly acknowledge that something is not right in our lives. Like Adam and Eve we would like to find a place to hide, or at least we would like to hide our weaknesses somewhere and pretend they do not exist. When we take a full view of ourselves, we find reasons for shame and embarrassment. Each of us is reminded daily of the fact that he is imperfect.

This recognition of our imperfections can add to our feelings of loneliness. The more we realize the weaknesses that live within ourselves, the more we may cower at the thought of being found out. For this reason, we build elaborate defensive structures and resist opening up completely. We want to keep our imperfections as secret as possible even if that detracts from our most trusted personal relationships.

There are some people who fail to confront themselves and accept the truth. As a result they deny their neediness and their loneliness; they live out their lives with a false sense of security and self-sufficiency. They are unlike those who are honest with themselves, acknowledging the empty hole on the inside and making an effort to fill that hole with a more God-centered lifestyle. In the struggle to overcome loneliness, all humans must recognize the imperfection within and the need for a lifesaving gift from God.

At this point you may be thinking: "This all sounds so pessimistic. It must be futile to try to escape our loneliness if it is so inevitable." Keep in mind that while it is true that loneliness is a fact of life for mortal man and each of us experiences it from time to time, *we need not give up in despair*. Loneliness does not have to be a burdening experience. We can use knowledge of our loneliness as a springboard to a greater appreciation for the gifts given to us by God. Notice how, in the following example, the awareness of loneliness actually serves to motivate:

As a middle-aged adult, Walter was prone to much self-analysis and finally began to come to grips with the loneliness that existed within him. Of all the people in the world, he never expected to discover that he was a lonely person. This discovery was not the result of a sudden, rude awakening; rather, it was a gradual process that came as Walter slowly found his own identity.

Walter's background was such that he had had little direct awareness of loneliness. His family was neither rich nor poor. His physical needs were always taken care of. His was a Christian home, so church activities and development of a spiritual life were a part of the family routine. He was led to Christ at the age of nine by his parents. With his outgoing personality Walter rarely had problems making friends and finding things to do with his spare time. His was a busy life filled with school and church activities, athletics, and music. Such busyness caused him to come in contact with a wide variety of people, so he usually knew of someone who would be willing to give him company whenever he wanted it. He rarely had time to consider what loneliness was or to do any in-depth thinking about sin.

Walter's early family life was not perfect by any stretch of the imagination, but it was generally carefree and fun. Each of the children in his family grew up with a reasonable measure of confidence and self-acceptance. One might say that they were the typical church-going, middle-class family. So the question arises: "How could someone who grew up in such a secure environment ever get to the point of feeling lonely?"

Walter's feelings of loneliness began to emerge when as an adult he started confronting some of the complacence with which he had been blocking out reality. He began to recognize that in his past it had been easy for him to disregard disappointments or troubled feelings because he somehow felt that life would not always be that way. He had always assumed that as an adult, when he would be calling his own shots and setting up his own ideal lifestyle, he would have few troubling and disappointing experiences. Maybe life wouldn't be perfect, but he assumed that he would always be able to reach out to someone close and overcome trouble spots quickly. (Can you remember ever thinking this way?)

Walter had had many naive notions about what adult independence would bring. He would surely sweep the girl of his dreams off her feet and enter into the most rewarding of relationships. He would be highly successful in his chosen profession as a bank officer. As a Christian he would set an example worth following. While these were admirable goals, there was one major problem: Idealism blunted his sense of realism.

Walter eventually met and married a fine woman who had all the characteristics he thought he needed. Like him, she too had come from a background that had solid values and emphasized the family unit. Perfect! At the same time he was already involved in a training program that seemed tailor-made for him. After the training program he moved on to a small but growing bank where his position was exactly what he had been striving for. During this time he was growing spiritually, taking an active role in church life. What more could he have wanted? It all seemed so storybook perfect.

But a gnawing sensation began in middle age when Walter realized that his life was not as storybook perfect as he wanted it to be. Something was not right. As he reflected on his past, he admitted that his family life had not been as ideal as he had wanted people to believe. His family had had difficulties just as everyone else, but he never wanted to admit them to anyone. He recognized that he had some lingering resentments regarding some of the mistakes his parents had made in bringing him up. Then he began to admit to himself that, though he had a good wife, there were times when they did not understand each other as he thought they should. In public he was able to put on a good show to make people think he had an excellent marriage. But in private he realized that he was not always a good husband.

Though Walter had developed solid relationships with his colleagues at work, he realized that they did not always know and understand the real Walter. He had friends scattered across the state, but long lapses of time would pass between visits. He began to admit that these friendships were not very close and that no one knew him 100 percent. This was something that did not sit well with him.

In addition, it seemed that no matter how much he continued to grow spiritually, he continued to sin. It was not comfortable knowing that he would always fall short of his ideal lifestyle. This discomfort with himself and his life circumstances was the root of his feeling of loneliness.

This feeling of loneliness did not seem right. A person who has had many positive experiences in life is not supposed to ever feel lonely. Or so Walter thought. Loneliness afflicts those who have just experienced the death of a spouse, or child, or parent. Or loneliness troubles the aged and handicapped who simply exist from one day to the next with little or no excitement, just hanging on. But Walter? Lonely? How could it be?

As Walter grappled more and more with his inner feelings, he began to reassess his views about life in general, and his purpose in life in particular. Simply recognizing that he was a person capable of loneliness caused Walter to begin searching for a genuine, fulfilling purpose in life. His search for the root of his loneliness caused him to begin the journey of getting to know himself in a fuller, more honest sense. It caused him to work in earnest to understand more fully the relationship that already existed between himself and God. He became more conscientious in his responsibilities as husband and father. He began to learn the art of patience in his social and business interactions. In short, by confronting the loneliness within, Walter began the process of changing his life.

SEVEN

THE VICTIMS OF LONELINESS—FROM YOUNG TO OLD

IT HAS ALREADY BEEN POINTED OUT that all of us at one time or another have faced circumstances that can cause loneliness. Although there have been relatively few extensive studies on loneliness, common sense tells us that loneliness affects each of us at some point in our lives. We have seen that loneliness is a mixed bag that has links to psychological, spiritual, and social factors.

Although there are some who deny it, each of us has at least two basic personal needs: (1) a need to feel loved and valued, and (2) a need to feel a sense of social belonging. Failure to meet either one of these needs makes us susceptible to lonely feelings. Failure to meet the first need is exemplified in the case of an individual who feels bad because he has been insulted or rejected by someone whose esteem he desires. Failure to meet the second need is exemplified in the case of a person who feels lost in a sea of people at a large public gathering. The loneliness of emotional isolation (the absence of love) is usually more painful than the loneliness of social isolation (the absence of a sense of belonging).

Since we each have different personalities and different social circumstances, our experiences of loneliness will differ, but the feeling is basically the same. Because of our personal imperfections and because of society's imperfections, we will all come face to face with this emotion during our lives. Even people with secure emotional attachments may feel intensely lonely when circumstances in their lives are not to their liking. There is nothing shameful about admitting loneliness. Loneliness is not necessarily an indication that there is something very wrong with a person. The more afraid we are of it, the more devastating it can be when it comes. While respecting it as a sign that things are not perfect in our world, we should remember that it is also a normal response to nonfulfillment of emotional and social needs.

How widespread is loneliness anyway? There is a common misconception that loneliness is a problem peculiar to the aged, or perhaps to shut-ins. While they certainly have bouts with loneliness, by no means do they have a corner on the market. Statistical information gathered in a telephone survey regarding the relationship between marital status and bouts with loneliness are of interest:

Among married people, 14 percent of the women and 9 percent of the men reported recent lonely feelings. It is not known whether married women actually do experience more loneliness or whether it is just easier for them to admit it.

Among single adults, 27 percent of the women and 23 percent of the men reported experiencing severe loneliness during the previous week.

Over 50 percent of the widowers surveyed reported experiencing loneliness in the preceding week, and 29 percent of the widows reported the feeling.

While the researcher did not survey an adequate number of divorced people to determine a specific percentage, they did tend to mention loneliness as the most common of their negative feelings.[1]

When you take into account that these statistics reflect the percentages of people who had experienced loneliness in the very recent past, the results are astounding. Depending on the study you read, anywhere from 11 percent to 26 percent of our national population have felt lonely within the past few weeks. This is a very high percentage. At some time or another each of us could include himself in that group.

You might want to take extra note of the fact that sex makes no substantial difference when it comes to avoiding loneliness. Because slightly more women than men admitted to loneliness in the foregoing survey, you might get the idea that loneliness is more a woman's problem. But don't forget that women are generally given more permission to express their feelings. Men may have a little more social freedom (being able to go more places without an escort, for example), but apparently they are no better at hiding from their feelings than are women. In fact, when you look at certain social tendencies, you might even conclude that men have more reason to feel lonely than women. For example, friendships with members of the same sex are usually more accessible to women than to men. And women are more likely to maintain close family ties. But regardless of sex or social circumstances, everyone is susceptible to loneliness. The rest of this chapter will examine how different groups of people are affected by loneliness.

Teenagers

It has been reported that of all people in our nation, the adolescent has the most problems with loneliness.[2] The teen years are the time in life when the need for social acceptance is at its peak. Adolescents regard themselves as no longer children, and most are making efforts to become more independent from their family. Ties with peer groups are extremely important. And the resulting pressure can be tremendous. Even if a teenager has a pleasant family atmosphere, loneliness can be a great problem if there are inadequate ties with other teens.

One of the most common problems experienced by teens is a feeling of being left out, of being a misfit. A teenager feels resentful when parents and teachers try to place restrictions on him as they would on a child. No teen wants to be treated like a child. Yet teenagers make awkward mistakes and errors in judgment when they try to act as adults. They just do not fit the adult category either. Caught between their own struggle to grow up and the inevitable dominance by adults, many teens wind up feeling like outcasts.

The teen years are also a time of questioning and idealism. Children simply mimic the words and attitudes of Mom and Dad regarding subjects such as politics or religion. But during the years when they are learning to deal with abstract concepts and being encouraged to think for themselves at school, many teens take on a crusader's view regarding complex social issues. They develop a critical mind-set with respect to the problems that adults have created in the world. Whatever the current popular idealistic thought among the peer group, many teens will blindly follow, thinking only in terms of surface solutions to the great questions of our times.

Annie is an example of how some young people respond to the pressures of the teen years. At seventeen she described herself as having had many rocky experiences from the time she had reached puberty. As a child she had been obedient, rarely giving her family any serious trouble. But when she reached thirteen, her desire to be liked by the in crowd caused her to get involved in activities that were not good for her.

One of Annie's friends, who had always been a daring person, enticed her into trying some marijuana. At first, they would smoke it and just giggle because they were doing something they considered grown-up. But as time went on, it became a habit; Annie felt she had to keep it up so her peer group would not make fun of her. She wanted so badly to be accepted by her peers that she allowed herself to get involved in deviant activities. It was that important to her.

Eventually common sense won out; by age sixteen Annie quit smoking marijuana. But when she did so, she faced the rejection of many of her old friends. This made her feel even more emotionally hungry for affection and caused her to cling to anyone, male or female, who would show an interest in her. She tried desperately to develop what she thought were mature, adult relations with these new friends. But in doing so, she put such intensity into her relationships that they would crumble under the strain.

During this time, Annie's parents tried to reach out to her, but in her prideful desire to be an adult, she rejected their appeals to her. When they eventually gave up on her, Annie could not understand why.

Since Annie saw herself as becoming an adult, pulling away from her family, she questioned virtually every major belief her parents held. She questioned the existence of God because she could not imagine how a loving God could create such a messed-up world. (She did not understand that humans are extremely skilled at defying God by misusing or abusing the many gifts He has made available to them.) She questioned her parents' political beliefs, developing radical, naive views of her own. She questioned their sense of morality and values, preferring to take on a me-oriented view of life. Eventually she became so pessimistic and critical in her thinking that she concluded life is not worth anything. A suicide attempt was nearly successful.

Annie's state of rebellion and disillusionment was all a result of the confusion she felt as she was trying to make the transition from childhood to adulthood, from dependence to independence. Teenagers who do not have proper guidance and understanding are very easily drawn into a lifestyle that guarantees loneliness. Because change and transitions are key experiences in the adolescent years, teens are easy prey for worldliness. Temptations seem to be at an all-time high during this stage of life since virtually every kind of experience is a new experience.

No one ever said that growing up would be easy. That is particularly true today since we have a far more permissive (and promiscuous) society than ever before. Thus, the possibility for loneliness in the teen years is greater than ever. Unfortunately, this problem does not just disappear as teens grow older. It can set into motion patterns that will reach far into adulthood.

Single Adults

We hear much more about the single-adult population today than we did twenty years ago. The reason is that there are more of them than ever before. In this century children have stayed dependent on their parents longer; one result is that as adults they tend to marry later. The booming of our highly technical society has caused more adults, male and female, to focus first on getting their careers off the ground and then on starting families.

This does not mean that emotional needs are put aside while these single adults are trying to climb the ladder of success. On the contrary, their emotional needs may actually be much stronger. While our culture emphasizes the value of getting ahead in the world, the individual still has a need for emotional attachment and support. While status-seeking may have its rewards, it can leave a person starved for love.

Ideally, of course, the strong need for love can be met in a marriage relationship: Marriage offers two people a chance to attain a level of intimacy unparalleled by any other type of relationship. Unfortunately for the single adult, the need for love must be filled some other way. Most singles will admit that one day they hope to be married. But in the meantime, they look for alternate ways to find emotional satisfaction.

In our culture, the single adult has at least one major obstacle to finding contentment. That is, our society is extraordinarily obsessed with erotic love. Finding this type of love is the ultimate dream that is drilled into our heads constantly. The vast majority of popular songs praise love, wail over love lost, or tell us we are nothing until we are wrapped in someone's arms. This can suggest to the single adult that he is incomplete without a physical love relationship. It is a brainwashing that never ends.

Because of this public obsession with physical love, single adults assume that it is not good enough just to have friends, workmates, or close family ties. Many are duped into believing that unless they have that one special relationship, they are emotional cripples. Consequently, many feel panicky about growing older without a spouse. Some will allow themselves to compromise their moral standards or do whatever it takes to find the right person.

For many, the search for love becomes the major focus of their lives. They flock to singles' bars on a regular basis, hoping their big chance will come and they will meet the person of their dreams. They fail to develop hobbies or outside interests for fear these interests will pull them out of the limelight. Love is their only hobby.

A twenty-seven-year-old woman complains that she is tired of looking for Mr. Right. She feels hypocritical because she knows the only reason she goes to church is to meet men. She hates blind dates, but she rarely turns one down in hopes that Mr. Right will be there. She dislikes the nightspots, but she can always be talked into going with her friends. "Beats sitting at home, and who knows who I'll meet?"

She wants to meet a man, get married, and settle down. In talking with her, one gets the impression that she will not see much of her friends after that because her future husband will be the sole recipient of her attention. Life will not begin until she finds him. No need to make any major plans for life until she finds him. No need to develop other interests; she is too busy looking for him. Friends are of secondary importance to her because she is looking for him.

What pressure! People like this may well be setting themselves up for serious disappointment and loneliness. There is little chance to be content with the present circumstances as long as a person is yearning for a future love. And to top it off, the intensity of this desire may result in making the wrong choice for a mate. So much emphasis is placed on finding *the* one. Many singles believe that their not having found *the* one is the primary cause of their loneliness.

Being realistic, we must admit that we are indeed a couple's culture. Women in particular feel very insecure about going out in public without an escort (though men suffer from this too). For example, how comfortable do you feel when you go to a restaurant by yourself? You would probably be more at ease if you were accompanied by someone. And if that someone were an attractive member of the opposite sex, it would be even better. No doubt, a single adult can feel out of place merely because of his single status. In our culture, this is fertile ground for loneliness to grow.

Married Adults

As we have mentioned, marriage is assumed to be the ultimate means of fulfilling the need to be loved and appreciated. But as common sense will tell us, when you put two imperfect people together, you are going to have an imperfect union. What happens to people who are not ready to face the imperfections of their marriage in a constructive way? You guessed it—they feel lonely, and they tend to blame each other.

When people get married to avoid the loneliness they are afraid of, they are adding a negative factor to their lives. Many people marry in order to defend themselves from being single, which they assume would be lonely. But when they learn that marriage is not a cure-all, their feelings of loneliness may be stronger than ever. Loneliness seems more severe when it occurs where least expected.

While marriage actually can provide the most intimate of relationships, it is not, as some would like it to be, the answer to all of our interpersonal problems. As young people look toward marriage, they see it as being a *final* solution to interpersonal needs. Actually, it is only a *beginning* in the quest for intimacy.

No doubt, marriage has many advantages that single life does not offer. In the survey cited earlier in this chapter, you may have noted that fewer married people reported lonely feelings than did singles. When people get married, they usually have an increased sense of belonging to someone and to the community. Married people tend to be in the leadership positions at church, in civic organizations, and in the business world. It can definitely be said that marriage has its advantages.

Yet seeds for loneliness can be planted in marriage as a result of some of the staggering expectations we may have for it. We imagine that marriage will completely remove any feeling of emptiness. We think: "There will be someone who will share my life with me, someone to love me, to care for me." This may be true, and certainly having our needs met can be one of the advantages of being married. But when a person's basic purpose for entering marriage is to have his needs met, there is a major problem. The focus of attention is on *me*, *my* needs, *my* dreams.

Such people may offer lip service to the notion of giving love to their partners. In fact, many will plan the majority of their activities around this notion of giving love to their partners. But this often covers the real reason for giving. Many are giving in order to receive. Of course, if you ask them if they give love only so they will receive love, most will deny it. But this is a hidden, unadmitted flaw in many a marriage.

Of course, not all people enter marriage merely for what they can get out of it. Many couples come together for very positive, mature reasons. The two of them both like and love one another. But because of the prevalent societal ideas regarding marriage, even these couples become disappointed if ultrahigh expectations are not met. Even the best relationships can be tested by work pressures, economic instabilities, and problems with children. For couples who came together for less than mature reasons (and this is usually the case), these pressures can be unbearable.

Persons who have high expectations for their marriage but find out later that these expectations are not attainable can be compared to a business executive who has to take a large cut in pay. If the executive is accustomed to a very high salary, an adequate salary seems paltry. It is very unsatisfactory. Likewise, if a couple marries in the belief that they are going to have the greatest of lives and will never experience any real worries, they too may come to the conclusion that their adequate, normal relationship is no good. This is not to say that couples should enter marriage expecting only mediocre results, nor that they should be satisfied with bland normalcy. It is meant as a warning that sky-high expectations can lead to intense loneliness if they are not met.

There is another factor that can cause loneliness in married life—an overemphasis on the couple's need for privacy. Have you ever noticed how many people will feel free to call on a single person late in the evening, while hesitating to call on a married person? We have a popular belief (and with good reason sometimes) that married couples are not supposed to be bothered. This becomes a problem when consideration for a couple's privacy is exaggerated.

Most couples want to be bothered if a friend or relative has a need. Yet people are often fearful to risk spontaneous or short-notice visits. Planning in advance can be overdone to the extent that social relations do not get the chance to develop beyond the stiff, formal stage.

Examples of our culture's emphasis on privacy are everywhere. Many housewives are reluctant to walk up to a neighbor's door and knock. They are afraid the neighbor might be too busy or perhaps just not in the mood for company. In truth, many are simply afraid of being turned away, even though there is little likelihood of that. Notice also how we are subtly encouraged to be reluctant to approach one another. In suburban neighborhoods, most yards have tall fences or hedges; we spend most of our free time indoors or away from the house; when we do see one another, we often only smile and wave rather than take a few minutes to chat. In short, we are very privacy-oriented. And while it is normal to have privacy in marriages, it can be overdone.

On a deeper level, it is often considered taboo for married persons to talk to others about anything negative in their married life. Teenagers can talk about their dates. Singles are allowed to discuss their feelings, but married people are not supposed to have problems. Marriage supposedly should have put an end to any confusion. You are in love, so you had better act as if you are. People who felt free to discuss problems previous to marriage keep their problems to themselves after marriage for fear of giving others the wrong impression. This adds pressure and intensifies negative feelings.

Overemphasis on the privacy of marriage adds to the notion that the marital relationship is the ultimate answer to interpersonal needs. We have seen that this discourages a couple from developing social relations and discussing their problems with others. While marriage truly is an institution of beauty, people should keep it in proper perspective, allowing themselves the chance to draw on other resources for personal satisfaction. No marriage can reach its full potential if one or both of the partners are looking exclusively to the other for satisfaction in life. That produces a pressure that will eventually yield undesirable results. Couples need to remain open to outside sources of satisfaction.

Parents

Many parents believe that their position in the family is a very thankless job. And justifiably so. As their children grow, parents are more than likely called upon to give far in excess of what they receive. To some, this is very gratifying because they see many positive events in their children's lives to make them feel that their efforts are worthwhile. But there are other parents who are not so fortunate.

Next to the husband-wife relationship, the parent-child bond is the strongest type of emotional involvement. In some instances in which the husband-wife relationship is weak, the parent-child bond is the closest involvement a person has with another human being. Parents tend to have high hopes that interaction with their children will bring them great joy. There is a strong desire to give and receive love. There is the hope that the child will provide many opportunities for parents to feel proud and satisfied about their family. Of course, this is all very normal.

But as in any relationship, there are imperfections or gaps between parents and children. Because parents have a natural love for their children, a feeling of emptiness can develop when children are not what they are supposed to be. Parents want badly to mold their children into respectable young men and women, but children do not always respond accordingly. Children have a tendency to want to go their own way and to make their own decisions. Many times the decisions that children make are so obviously wrong that it is almost unbearable for parents to live with those mistakes.

Virtually all parents are well-intentioned toward their children from the time of their birth. As an infant enters their life, parents pledge to themselves to be loving and understanding toward the child. They vow to maintain solid, open lines of communication with the child. But as the child grows, flaws emerge in the parent-child relationship, and parents are often left questioning where they went wrong. They wonder why a distance exists between themselves and the young ones they love so dearly. When parents feel lonely, they have fallen victim to the ugly reality of separateness between imperfect humans.

Helen and Ron were considered by their friends and associates to be highly conscientious parents. Their two children were considered among the best mannered in the school. Both were popular with their classmates and had friends over at the house frequently. In a word, their household was pleasant. But one day Helen and Ron got the alarmingly bad news that their nine-year-old son had been caught stealing from the local drugstore. They never would have expected this from such a previously well-behaved child. "Why would he need to do this? Didn't he know that if he wanted something he could simply ask us for it?" It just did not make sense.

When Helen and Ron asked their son about this, all he could say was that he did not know why he did it; he just did it. A sense of deep hurt came over them when they were forced to admit that their child was not as perfect as they wanted to believe. Though they wanted a close-knit family, they realized that there would be other such instances that would stand in the way of the desired unity. In other words, it was painfully evident that there was a separateness in the family.

Parents may have such a strong desire for their children to succeed that they may unconsciously be setting themselves up for bitter disappointments. Rather than accepting the fact that there will always be flaws, they put pressure on the family to be perfect. And even when they do accept the fact of imperfections, it is still difficult to live with it. Because the bond is so great between parent and child, the loneliness can be extreme when things do not go according to plans.

Divorced Persons

Divorce is affecting far more people today than ever before. We are seeing half as many divorces as marriages.

Before the twentieth century, divorce was highly unusual. It was simply understood that when people married, it was for life. Now many couples take the attitude that if the marriage does not work, divorce is always a ready solution. There are far less stringent attitudes regarding marriage, and unfortunately many are reaping the results.

Divorce can be one of the loneliest of life's experiences. A person in the process of divorce is being forced to give up a dream, the dream that two people who felt they were in love could live in a mutually satisfying relationship. When something for which one originally had high hopes eventually fails, the consequences can be bitterly painful. Divorced persons often feel very defensive about their failure. It seems to separate them from "normal" people.

Perhaps the greatest difficulty divorced persons face is their sense of being a failure. They believe that they are branded losers because of their crumbled marriage. One divorced man remarked that he felt as if there was a big "F" tattooed in the middle of his forehead for everyone to see. Divorced persons realize they have missed the mark. They have not achieved the ideal they were supposed to. Even though they realize that other people have failures too, they feel that their failure is worse.

When a person gets divorced, there is a completely new lifestyle to adjust to. For some it may mean coming home to an empty house, eating alone, sleeping alone. For others it may mean getting back in the job market, taking care of the children by oneself, using inadequate day-care facilities. And for most, there are usually financial adjustments, whether it be making child-support payments or losing a spouse's good income. The adjustment to an unfamiliar way of life is not easy.

Divorced persons usually welcome emotional support from outside sources. But even then problems can occur. Often friends are forced to choose sides, causing further resentments. In addition, most of those people who have recently been divorced feel like a fifth wheel with a group of couples. And when a couple does invite a divorced person out, he or she suspects that they are only trying to do the nice thing and would rather not have to extend themselves to a half-person. Though friends may seem well-intentioned, divorced people often are suspicious of their invitations and offers of support. It is difficult to graciously accept someone else's support when a person has less than complete acceptance of himself because of his feelings of guilt and low self-esteem.

And then, divorced persons have their families to contend with. Remember, divorce is a growing social phenomenon. That means it was not as prevalent when our parents grew up. And certainly it was almost unheard-of during our grandparents' days. As a result, families have not had much previous experience in dealing with divorce. Although it varies with the individual family, divorced persons may find that family support is not as strong as they would like. Often they tried to keep the marital problems as hidden as possible from the family. When the situation finally came out into the open, the response was surprise or even criticism rather than support. Divorce does not simply bring pain to the parties immediately involved. The family has feelings to deal with too, and until their own feelings are sorted out, some have a hard time offering their understanding to the one who needs it the most.

There are so many upsetting factors in a divorce situation that it is virtually impossible to go through the experience without having painful emotions. The problems of these painful emotions are greatest during the hours one normally would have spent with a partner. There are special times such as Christmas, birthdays, or just mealtimes when the sense of loss seems most acute. Once a person has tasted the good life, it is hard to live with the aftereffects of splitting up.

Unresolved emotions usually cause the painful, lonely feelings to persist. For example, it is common for the wife who has to get a job while taking care of three children to feel angry because her ex-husband is living carefree by himself with far fewer responsibilities. Or perhaps a husband feels resentful because his chances for getting ahead in business are hampered due to his divorced status. When these types of feelings fester, the chance for loneliness increases. They cause the individuals to maintain the focus on self, rather than reaching out in a giving manner to others.

Those who learn to overcome the loneliness of divorce are usually the ones who are able to maintain an optimistic view of the future. Some of these people are humble enough to admit to themselves that they had a role in the marital problems, meaning that they have areas in their lives that need improvement. Those who do not seek to eliminate weaknesses in self are asking for a long-term bout with loneliness.

The Elderly

The problem of loneliness during the latter years of life potentially affects 10 percent of our national population. Since life expectancy is on the rise, a great proportion of our nation's people will in the near future be forced to contend with the problems unique to the older generation. Longevity can certainly have its rewards, but it can cause problems too.

Ours is a culture that values the work ethic. This means that idleness is looked upon with scorn. Yet many people find that once they reach the age of retirement, idleness comes easily, perhaps too easily. Because of this, elderly citizens can lose self-respect and may feel that the younger population does not have a very high level of regard for them. One man in his seventies explained to us that he had had inferiority feelings in his younger days, but those feelings increased dramatically once he stopped work to settle into a life of retirement. He felt that he was useless to people, simply in the way.

Our rapidly changing society is all too ready to place older people on the back shelf. We are living in an age when knowledge often becomes obsolete in a matter of years. Consequently, we look to the fresh, inventive type of person who is up to date on the latest developments in his field of work. Youth is desirable; age means one is behind the times. Consequently, older citizens are no longer looked up to as the holders of wisdom. In our day, it is not considered important that we look to them as preservers of tradition. Youth is in. In our fast-paced world, the elderly can quickly lose their sense of worth to the community. As it seems, they are quite replaceable.

Losing one's position in the community, and the respect that goes along with it, can bring a loss of self-esteem. When a person has strived all his life to achieve some recognition in his chosen profession only to lose it in his later years, he may feel as though the heart of his personal identity has been taken away. In a world in which people are judged by their performance, someone who no longer performs has nothing to stand on. Rather than being known as a banker, or salesman, or teacher, he may simply be known as a retiree. To many, this signifies staleness, nonproductivity. It means that a person is choosing merely to lie back and let others do the work. Or so it seems.

An additional problem that quite often comes with age is a lowered standard of living. Not all retirees have investments to fall back on or a generous pension plan. With loss of income comes a loss of opportunity to do enjoyable things. While many people look forward to the time when they no longer have to work and can enjoy doing whatever they wish, the sad truth is that our nation's economic system often does not allow ordinary pleasures. For example, a cross-country trip that might have been affordable ten years ago may no longer be possible for many elderly people. Even the simplest pleasures, such as eating out at a restaurant, can put a strain on a tight, fixed budget. When people are forced to stay at home for financial reasons, boredom sometimes sets in. This, of course, is fertile ground for loneliness.

Another problem faced by the elderly is loss of physical capabilities. Some of the loss may be gradual, but some can come rather suddenly. We know of an elderly man who had worked with his hands all of his life; he had been very adept at some of the small manual chores around the house. But he developed Parkinson's disease, which causes a loss of muscular control, and he felt sorely deficient in his ability to do some of the menial tasks that had once come so easily. Others experience poorer eyesight or hearing, stiffening of the joints, or slower gait. Often these problems come when a person is not expecting them, a fact that only makes matters worse.

Keeping in mind that ours is a society that stresses the beauty of youth, many elderly people feel bad about the deterioration of their physical attributes. Because we have learned to be vain about our appearance, many are disturbed by unhidable wrinkles, loss of hair, age spots. Serving as a reminder that they are out of step with the younger generation, physical deterioration disturbs some older folks quite badly.

It is also a fact of life that as we grow older there are more chances to witness death. The death of a spouse or a close friend can cause a person to feel lost in the world. As time passes, elderly people learn of the deaths of persons who once made life enjoyable for them. Death can be a bleak reminder of the temporary nature of relationships. Of all the potential problems facing the elderly, the death of loved ones is usually the most severe.

To sum up the situation for the older generation: While they continue to face some of the trying circumstances their younger counterparts face, they have additional problems as well. But don't misunderstand. The aged are not doomed to a life of loneliness and despair. But there are extra pressures for the person who does not prepare adequately in advance.

EIGHT

THE CHILDREN OF LONELINESS

PEOPLE OFTEN ASK, "Why does a loving God allow us to experience loneliness and its unpleasant consequences?" By asking such a question, they are virtually blaming God for all of the evil and suffering in the world. This is not an easy question to answer.

When God created man, He created him perfect. Man did not originally have any sin or loneliness in him. But because God did not want to create a puppet or a machine, man had the choice to obey or disobey God. Had man obeyed God there would be no such thing as loneliness. We all would have an unending life of fellowship with God and enjoyment of His creation. But since the first man sinned, we have all been born into a life of sin. And since we all have continued the progression of sin, we must each suffer its consequences.

But why didn't God make us so we would not sin? He could have; but if He had, we would not be human beings. We would be like a talking doll that says, "I love you," when we pull its string. Our relationship with God would have no depth or meaning. Apparently, God thought that it was worth the risk to create us as we are. We have brought sin into our lives as a choice, and we are left to face the consequences. Ultimately, however, God will stamp out evil and restore the believing Christian to the original perfect state.

Until we are restored to that perfect state, we will continue to suffer loneliness and its consequences. That is part of being human. As we have already seen, there are three basic causes for loneliness: (1) lack of intimacy with God, (2) lack of intimacy with others, and (3) lack of self-worth. This chapter will explore the children (the consequences) of chronic loneliness.

Feeling out of Fellowship with God

Because of our human imperfections, we are bound to fall short of a state of constant communion with God. However, it is possible to feel a sense of consistency and security when there is a well-established relationship with God through Jesus Christ. Unfortunately, the person who suffers from loneliness does not allow himself to grasp the inner peace found in this relationship. Recognition of his sinfulness causes him to retreat from God due to feelings of shame and embarrassment (as Adam and Eve did).

With this frame of mind, it's easy to have misconceptions of who God is. It is heartbreaking to hear people accuse God of being evil on the grounds that He brings sin and its consequences into the lives of innocent victims here on earth. (Keep in mind that God did not choose for us to sin; we did!) Because God does not immediately remove certain circumstances from people's lives, many assume that it is His desire that we should suffer. In their minds, God is cold and heartless. To them, God is a mean old man holding a whip.

Many others cannot understand how God can despise the sin in our lives, yet warmly invite us to have fellowship with Him. It seems inconsistent. Apparently they are not convinced that Christ's death was sufficient to restore us to right fellowship with God. But the fact is that the suffering and death of Christ was a final event that never needs to be repeated. The person who succumbs to the burden of loneliness is attempting to shoulder the weight of his own imperfections rather than handing it over to the atoning Savior. Each time he becomes preoccupied with his imperfections, he feels farther away from God, assuming that God on His throne is shaking His head in thorough disgust.

We may *feel* out of fellowship with God, but the simple truth is that once Christ comes into our hearts, He is there to stay. A person who chronically suffers from spiritual loneliness either is not a Christian, or he is a Christian who is not fully in touch with the saving grace of God that exists in him in the person of Jesus Christ.

Constant Guilt Feelings

Guilt feelings are usually accompanied by thoughts such as, "I should perform more capably"; "I am a failure"; "I wish I were someone else." The Bible does not encourage this type of guilt feeling. A nagging feeling of guilt is one of the major causes of the feeling of separation from God. You may wonder, "But how can a sinful person be honest with himself without feeling guilty?" The answer lies in a comprehensive understanding of guilt.

There are two types of guilt, objective guilt and subjective guilt. Objective guilt is based on facts. It is a fact that we do things that are wrong. Objective guilt is based on recognition that we break certain laws, whether they are society's laws or God's laws. Regardless of what we feel, the Bible clearly teaches that we are all sinful and imperfect because we break God's laws in both thought and action. There is no doubt, objectively, that we are all guilty before God. This is also known as *true guilt*.

Subjective guilt is the unhealthy *feeling* of negativism we harbor toward ourselves when we recognize our objective guilt. It is based on a negative judgment we make concerning ourselves. It is accompanied by thoughts such as, "God won't love me as much"; "What if people knew what I am really like?"; "I don't like who I am." We can be objectively guilty without experiencing subjective guilt. Subjective guilt is an unnecessary feeling brought on by persistent feelings of loneliness and self-condemnation.

It is important for us to understand the Bible's teaching on how to handle guilt. Consider the following example from John 8:1–11:

> But Jesus went to the Mount of Olives. And early in the morning He came down again into the temple, and all the people were coming to Him; and He sat down and began to teach them. And the scribes and the Phar-

> isees brought a woman caught in adultery, and having set her in the midst, they said to Him, "Teacher, this woman has been caught in adultery, in the very act. Now in the Law Moses commanded us to stone such women; what then do You say?" And they were saying this, testing Him, in order that they might have grounds for accusing Him. But Jesus stooped down, and with His finger wrote on the ground. But when they persisted in asking Him, He straightened up, and said to them, "He who is without sin among you, let him be the first to throw a stone at her." And again He stooped down and wrote on the ground. And when they heard it, they began to go out one by one, beginning with the older ones, and He was left alone, and the woman, where she had been, in the midst. And straightening up, Jesus said to her, "Woman, where are they? Did no one condemn you?" And she said, "No one, Lord." And Jesus said, "Neither do I condemn you; go your way; from now on sin no more." (NASB)

Jesus did not try to make this woman feel bad (guilty). Undoubtedly she felt bad enough as it was. He knew that if He increased the woman's frustrations by labeling her a bad person, she would be driven away from the experience of God's love.

Low Self-Esteem

When we lack fellowship with God and experience degrading guilt feelings, we seem to have very little basis for feeling good about who we are. Self-esteem is a recognition that there is value and worth in ourselves.

A person with low self-esteem is one who feels inadequate as a person, insignificant, and worth very little.

Individuals who feel the insecurity of low self-esteem have numerous experiences of anxiety, suspicion, and doubt. They are overly concerned about their abilities, judgment, and goals. They question their own feelings and decisions. Because they experience such uncertainty, they expect others to have negative thoughts about them, and this only worsens the situation. They assume that no matter what they do, rejection will be waiting for them.

Not all individuals who have a sense of low self-esteem look lonely. Some people become very skilled at developing surface relationships that give the impression of stability and inner peace. They become experts at hiding their true identity and their true feelings. They may have many acquaintances but few (if any) real friends. Some are so skilled that they are able to minister to the needs of others, yet they will allow no one to minister to them for fear that they will be found out.

Let us illustrate: Sarah was a young woman in her late twenties who was liked by her peers and social acquaintances. She had special musical talents that she used in church worship services. She played the piano, sang in the choir, helped with children's work. Seemingly, she had it all together.

The reason she came to our office was that she found herself feeling panicky whenever she would perform in front of people, even if it was something as routine and unnoticeable as being one of sixty choir members. As we discussed her problems, we found that at the root of her panic was a feeling of low self-esteem. Sarah was afraid that she might make a mistake in front of people and they would laugh. Whenever she looked into her personality, she saw one weakness after another. She was so sensitive to her weaknesses that she feared she would be readily rejected by others. This all stemmed from her parents, who accepted her only on condition that she perform well. As a result, she hid her mistakes and blamed herself for not being acceptable.

Sometimes these inferiority feelings are very obvious and sometimes they are quite subtle. If one will be honest with himself, recognizing his tendency toward sin, he will admit that there are legitimate reasons to feel inferior. After all, because of sin we have fallen from the superior creation that man originally was. The problem comes when people focus so heavily on their imperfections that they assume there is little reason for others to accept them.

An awkward feeling can overcome a person when he is a newcomer, or outsider, who tries his best to feel at home among a group of people who have known one another for a long time. Imagine yourself in this situation. Everyone else in the room may be laughing about old times or talking about common interests. But when the conversation turns to you, all they can think of to ask is, "Where are you from? Have you lived here long? What kind of work do you do?" There is an uneasy realization that you are different. You are not a part of the in crowd.

We usually have a sense of inferiority at times like this. We can rationally tell ourselves that these other people are no better or worse than we are, but in truth, the feeling is there anyway. For a person with a reasonable amount of self-confidence, this feeling will not be too long-lived. But for the person who persistently grapples with loneliness this feeling can be painful.

Too often, people confuse being different with being inferior. A person might find that he does not share other people's interests and therefore might assume there is something wrong with him. Or perhaps he might see that another person has far superior skills in a particular area and again draw the conclusion that he himself is inferior.

Inferiority feelings do not generally pop up overnight. They usually have their origins in childhood. For example, it is easy for a child to get the message that he is inferior unless he makes A's and B's on his report card. Or it is easy for a child to feel inferior if he is the one who strikes out most on his little-league team. Usually adults have no intention of making a child feel inferior, but our culture is so performance-conscious that this is often the result. Even children who excel in virtually everything can have inferiority feelings because of a dread fear of failing.

A sense of loneliness can cause these feelings of inferiority to come to the forefront of our minds. A single adult may feel lonely due to a desire to be married, and he may question why no one loves him well enough to marry him. A divorced person, feeling the loneliness of separation from a spouse and from former friends, may feel like a failure, like someone who is not good enough, a reject. A businessman who does not fit well in the corporate structure may conclude that others are better or more favored than he.

What these people fail to remember is that in God's eyes there is no person who is favored over another. Some may have a closer walk with Him, and some may work more fervently for Him. But He loves us all just the same. As far as He is concerned, we all are in the same class—persistent sinners who need His love and His plan for atonement. We have no business judging ourselves to be inferior. Though we are all different, in a sense we are all the same.

Let's imagine a swimming competition. The two contestants are you (the reader) and Mark Spitz, the record-setting Olympic gold medalist. The competition is to see who can swim first to Japan, starting from the coast of California. Mark Spitz and you start together on the California coast, and he takes the lead from the very start. You experience trouble with the surf and have to roll over on your back many times due to your early exhaustion. Soon, after having gone but a short distance, you have to be dragged out of the water.

Meanwhile, Mark Spitz is swimming along at a nice clip. It takes a long time for him to get weary. He paces himself well, using the backstroke when necessary, and he is able to get much farther than you. But eventually he, too, tires. And the same boat that picked you up has to pull him out of the water as well. In the final results, you both are pitifully short of your destination, and you both have the exact same need for salvation.

Such is the case in life. There are many who feel as though they are accomplishing very little while they watch others pass them by with ease and a seeming lack of effort. But to say one person is inferior to another because he has not had as many successes is folly. We can trick ourselves into believing that there is such a thing as inferiority to other people, but in reality God declares each human to be uniquely significant (see Ps. 139).

Exaggerated Feelings of Dependency

Chronically lonely people have two strikes against them when it comes to developing meaningful relationships. By refusing to accept some of the basic realities of life, these people cling to the thought that an ideal life does exist somewhere. Their burning desire for this ideal life causes them to distort what is real and to become disappointed when their dreams fail to come true. Such an approach to life can place tremendous pressure on relationships.

There is no doubt that God created us to be interdependent people. We can readily see that dependence is inborn in all of us. A tiny infant is totally dependent on his parents to feed, bathe, and clothe him. He is also dependent on his parents to love and nurture him. Of course, as time progresses, it is natural for the child to learn to do things independently. The closer he gets to adulthood, the more independent he should be. This does not mean that as adults we should expect ourselves to be completely independent from one another. On the contrary, we still have dependency needs. We still need to know that someone in this world loves us. But at the same time, it is important for each of us to achieve an appropriate balance between dependency and independency.

People who have constant bouts with loneliness often fall into the overly dependent style of life. Because they feel lonely, they seem desperate to hear from someone that they are loved. They tell themselves they cannot have a sense of peace and contentment until they are convinced there are people who love them.

An overly dependent person not only wants to feel loved and accepted (which is normal) but also must absolutely have it in order to feel stable. He becomes excessively distraught if he is rejected by someone. Yet he tends toward disbelief when people do show love and support. He clings to people, sucking up all their emotional energy. He is unaware of the potential strength that lies within himself to make the most out of life and to withstand trying times.

Lonely persons are constantly looking for the perfect relationship, hoping that it will simply be a matter of time before things fall into place. But it never comes. Instead of being realistic, they expect that they themselves and those around them will live in such a way that there will never be any disappointments or sadness. When disappointments do occur, they become distraught. They place even heavier expectations on others. They are depending on others to pull them through, to fulfill their hopes and dreams for a satisfying life.

Dependent persons tend to follow a predictable progression in their relationships. They first *discount* their own abilities to take charge of their emotional lives. Second, they *expect* others to fulfill their needs for them. Then they begin to *make demands* of those on whom they depend. Naturally, this causes others to retreat from them, keeping at a distance. The dependent person finds himself back at square one and usually continues the cycle endlessly.

This discount-expect-demand cycle often is so subtle that people are unaware of what is happening. They are aware only of their unhappiness, their disillusionment, their loneliness. Here is an example: John came into our counseling office complaining of difficulty at home with his wife and two children. He had been married for fourteen years and had never felt satisfied with the relationships within his family. As we explored his difficulties, John began admitting to himself that he had always had uneasy feelings about himself. He would *discount* himself. That is, he did not give himself credit for being a good father and husband. He then realized how this caused him to *expect* many things from his wife and children. He expected his wife to be demonstrative in her love for him. This would give him the confidence he sorely lacked. After all, he was the main provider and she should be appreciative of his efforts to maintain a home. He expected his children to show respect and appreciation for his efforts as their father. He thought that anyone as good to his children as he was ought to receive adequate demonstrations of regard at home. Since he did not believe that he was a good husband and father, he wanted to hear it from his family.

Without knowing it, John had become dependent on his family for his feelings of worth and value. When his expectations were not met in the manner that he wanted, he would sometimes become depressed. This depression prodded him toward making increased *demands* of his family for better behavior and more displays of affection and unity. To his dismay, he would get the opposite result. His wife became less demonstrative of her love. His children showed less respect and seemed to be afraid of him, shying away from him on many occasions.

Until counseling, John had not understood that his expectations and demands were a result of strong dependency needs. Furthermore, he was refusing to accept some very basic facts. He had not accepted the fact that, while he and his wife would sometimes relate to one another with differing styles, these differing styles did not automatically mean they had a bad marriage. He had also refused to accept the fact that his children were quite capable of being imperfect and that their misbehavior did not mean he was a bad parent. Consequently, he found himself feeling more and more separate from his family, yet clinging more and more desperately. This was exactly the opposite of what he wanted.

Many people, like John, will not give themselves permission to feel good about themselves until their value has been confirmed by others. Like John, they want very much to have respect for themselves but wait for others to bestow it first.

Harsh, Critical Feelings

Lonely people are not always the quiet, withdrawn types. Loneliness can cause angry, rebellious feelings. Not all people respond to loneliness by simply cowering from the crowd. Many want to strike back. Perhaps one of the most common ways for a person to compensate for his lonely feelings is to develop a critical attitude.

We all have heard the expression, "Misery loves company." To some extent, it is this kind of attitude that lies behind the critical nature. When people feel wronged, separated from others, there is a tendency to want to pull others down with them. What could be a better way to drag others down than to start finding faults in them?

The critical nature has close connections with inferiority feelings. The feeling of inferiority is a result of loneliness. Since none of us likes feeling inferior all the time, we tend to go through life trying to prove ourselves superior in some unique way. A critical nature can make a person feel falsely superior. It can temporarily cover up the inner feelings of loneliness. By being critical, a person can convince himself that his loneliness is not his fault and that everything would be better if other people would just do what they are supposed to do. This is a widely used excuse for not taking responsibility for one's own life.

Here is an example: Joan was a middle-aged woman who complained that she had a very unhappy marriage. When she got married she had thought that her husband was nigh onto perfect. She couldn't have been happier. But as time went on, she felt more and more uncomfortable with the little differences that existed between herself and her husband. She began to feel lonely and separate; unfortunately her solution to her problem was to try to make her husband fit the mold she had in mind for him. She developed a critical attitude.

In public, Joan would scold her husband for not standing up straight. Though he held a responsible job and provided well for the family, she would nag him that he should have been a doctor. When he dressed to go out for the evening, she would complain that he wore the wrong color of socks. When he took off early from work, she would complain that he didn't work hard enough. When he worked late, she would criticize him for not being home.

The saddest part of this illustration is that Joan held firmly to the belief that if only her husband would live as she wanted him to live, they could have a happy marriage. She felt lonely because her marriage was not exactly as she wanted. But her response to her loneliness was to put the burden of change on someone else. In the final analysis she was too afraid to try to make changes for fear that her efforts would not be good enough (inferiority feelings).

If nothing else, a critical nature can give a lonely person a temporary feeling of smugness by thinking his problem is someone else's fault. He may give intellectual assent to the idea that he is at least in part responsible for his loneliness. But simply placing the blame on other people offers a good way out. This can momentarily ease lonely feelings, but in the long run it causes these feelings to continue since criticism only heightens separation.

Living according to Absolutes

We have already determined that loneliness, or separateness, is a fact of life, since we are sinners. In the last part of this book we will see that there are several biblically based steps a person can take to overcome the harmful effects of loneliness. But some people try to take the problems of their sinful nature into their own hands, developing a style of living based on a system of man-made or self-imposed absolutes. They foolishly try to convince themselves that by laying absolutes in front of themselves they stand a better chance of overcoming the problems their sinful lives can bring.

There are some key words that can tip us off that we are trying to build a life based on rigid absolutes. For example, how often do we use words such as "have to," "must," "should," "are supposed to," "ought to," and "had better"? Without knowing it, we can build an entire lifestyle around these words and in the process actually hamper our efforts to overcome problem areas in our lives.

Of course, the Bible does give us many absolute directives and commandments from God. It is not a book of "maybe's." And we certainly are to strive as best as we can to fulfill the directives that Scripture lays down.

On the other hand, there is a danger in building a life around personal or even parental absolutes. We might fool ourselves into thinking that we can *work* ourselves into perfection. When we continually use words such as "must" in reference to our own actions and behavior, we are implying that we have no choice. There is only one way to live. Nothing else will suffice. Nothing else is acceptable. There is no freedom.

Do you recall with whom Jesus had the most trouble in His earthly ministry? It was the religious leaders. And the reason He had constant differences with them is that they lived by a strict "must system." They had one law after another spelling out what people should do or should not do. Jesus had no quarrel with the fact that they had rules. He was a disciplined person Himself. What bothered Him was that these religious leaders were so intent on keeping rules that they overlooked human emotions and were intolerant of human frailties.

Without knowing it, when people experience loneliness they come up with absolutes they think will cure them of their distress. A single woman may say, "I *have to* have a husband before I can feel content." Parents may say to a child in whom they are disappointed, "You *must* behave better if you want us to love you." A college student may cry out, "People *shouldn't* be so fickle. They *ought* to treat me better."

Absolutes imply perfection. But there is not a perfect person on earth. By insisting that things work out perfectly, we are actually setting ourselves up for continued discouragement and loneliness. We are only giving ourselves false hope by holding on to the thought that life's problems would be completely erased if only we could perform as we know we *must*, or if others would perform as they *should*.

It is quite easy to see how a person can come to live by absolutes. Ours is a society that emphasizes and highlights the *ideal* life. Each family has its own way of passing on its conception of what the ideal life is. Sometimes it is passed on in a very clear-cut manner, and sometimes it is done subtly. Some families place a high value on academic achievement, some on athletic abilities, others on artistic skills. Certain personality traits, such as aggression, may be encouraged in one home and discouraged in another.

As we grow, we become indoctrinated with the ideals of our culture. The advertising media are quick to capitalize on our desire to be the ideal person. So they present their products to us in a way that makes us feel incomplete unless we buy what they tell us to buy. In addition, we come to idolize certain entertainers, businessmen, and politicians. We learn that an outgoing personality makes one very popular, and we prize a quick wit or a high level of intelligence.

This chapter has shown that loneliness breeds feelings and behaviors that are out of balance. Loneliness is at the root of a lot more problems than we once realized. We close this chapter with an illustration of what happened to a young woman who allowed herself to be swallowed up by the feeling of loneliness. Several of the consequences of loneliness discussed in this chapter were manifest in her life.

Carolyn was a woman in her late twenties who came to our psychiatric clinic with the complaint that she and her husband, Lewis, had difficulty demonstrating affection to one another. She said that she and Lewis seemed able to talk about anything and everything. In fact, their verbal communication seemed to be as open and direct as that of most couples who have solid marriage relationships. But there was something wrong that caused them to feel a great sense of emptiness and separateness when they were together.

Carolyn assumed that she simply had some misconceptions about sex and that as soon as they were cleared up, her marriage would be whole. But there was a great deal of inner turmoil that she was not expressing. We learned that Carolyn had grown up in a small farming community that offered very few modern conveniences. The nature of her family life was sad indeed. Her father seemed to be well-intentioned with respect to fulfilling his role as the leader of the family, but he was sorely lacking in interpersonal skills. He was extremely autocratic and stern, ruling the roost by instilling fear in his family. Each member of the family had been afraid to differ with him. He had set his own unwavering standards for the family, and all the family members felt they had to measure up to his ideal before he would consider them acceptable or worth loving.

Carolyn's family was very religious, following their personal interpretation of the Bible in a very diligent manner. Even though her father seemed harsh and unloving, it was understood that he was still the head of the household and she must never question his actions or his motives. In Carolyn's view this meant that even daring to think an angry thought or doing something he would not approve of was bad. She learned very emphatically that being herself was wrong. She felt very guilty if she ever questioned her father or experienced what she considered to be inappropriate sentiments toward him. She constantly feared that she was not measuring up to the proper standards. She felt lonely most of the time.

As Carolyn grew into adulthood, it was natural for her to want to conform to the ways of the people she respected, just as she had done with her father. Any thoughts, feelings, or opinions that might be considered contrary to their standards she would try to blot out of her mind. If she ever experienced anger or rebelliousness, she felt guilty. Whatever the crowd did, she would do. She thought she knew what type of person she should be, but she did not have the insight to realize how much of a burden that was.

As you might have guessed, Carolyn's feelings began to overwhelm her. She felt tremendously unfulfilled in her pursuit of the ideal life. It never seemed to bring her happiness. Her life was a constant struggle leaving her disillusioned with who she was. By the time she came to our clinic she was feeling cheated in life, estranged from virtually everyone she had ever known. She had unconsciously begun to despise her marriage with Lewis since she was overwhelmed by her conviction that she was supposed to be the perfect wife. She harbored many deep-seated feelings of resentment toward family members and friends; it was hard to think anything good about them. She felt as though God cared very little about her, or else He would have given her a better environment in which to grow up.

Can you imagine the deep loneliness Carolyn felt on countless occasions throughout her life? She had never had a balanced picture of herself and of life. Her tendency was to see things as being either all good or all bad. Since she knew that she was not all good and since she had learned that the world was not all good, she had only one conclusion to draw. Everyone everywhere was bad. Naturally this perpetuated her loneliness until she finally resolved her conflicts through several months of intensive therapy.

While loneliness can bring many unfortunate consequences, we need not just give up in pessimism. By understanding how loneliness can affect our lives, we can rise above the problem.

NINE

THE COUSINS OF LONELINESS

THERE ARE VARIOUS WAYS of showing loneliness. It is incorrect, then, to assume that loneliness always manifests itself in a quiet, withdrawn mood. Loneliness is generally considered to represent the dark side of human nature. As a result, other dark feelings can accompany it. In fact, loneliness is often masked by feelings of anger, or depression, or some other negative emotion. Loneliness is one of the root causes of many of the other painful emotions we are confronted with. This chapter will examine these cousins of loneliness.

Anger

On the surface, loneliness and anger seem to be unrelated, to stem from different origins. Anger seems more of an explosive type of emotion, while loneliness seems more of an inner, hidden emotion. Yet anger is sometimes closely related to loneliness, particularly when the anger is born of rebellion, vindictiveness, or bitterness.

A teenager whom we will call Bob would never admit that he felt lonely. He was very aware, though, of an excessive amount of anger within himself. At fifteen years of age Bob had never felt close to anyone in his life. Those who meant the most to him seemed unable to give him understanding and support in a way that would make him feel he was someone of significance. Bob's parents had always been well-intentioned toward him, but they were sorely lacking in interpersonal skills. Consequently, Bob grew up with a poor sense of self-esteem. Deep inside was a painful feeling that he was worthless and unloved.

Rather than simply accepting the notion that he was worthless, Bob made an unconscious decision at an early age to fight back. He would argue and act stubborn whenever his parents or teachers tried to fit him into their mold. He was rude and inconsiderate toward his classmates and playmates because deep down he was afraid that they did not think very highly of him. So he struck out at them first in order to lessen the pain of isolation.

Behind the anger, Bob was trying to make a brash statement to the world: "Maybe you don't think I'm worth anything, but I'll show you that I'm someone! I don't need you anyway!" Feeling separated from all other people, he wanted to believe he was still powerful. He was still *someone*. He was presenting himself as a superior, self-sufficient person in an attempt to hide from his true feelings of loneliness.

When most of us get angry, we do not go to quite the extreme that Bob did. But anger frequently surfaces at those times when something happens to cause us to feel separated, isolated, or unappreciated. For example, our colleagues at work may ignore us when we are trying to communicate something important. At that point, we feel separated, as though our colleagues were saying, "You're not important; don't bother us." Or perhaps we are trying to explain why we made certain decisions, and our spouse refuses to accept our way of thinking. Anger is our immediate response to the sense of isolation (loneliness) that has suddenly appeared. In essence, through our anger we are trying to communicate, "Accept me! Notice that I am significant, whether you agree with me or not."

We can become so oversensitive to the separation between ourselves and other people that anger can exhibit itself at very inappropriate times. For example, have you ever gotten mad and stayed mad simply because someone pulled out in front of you unexpectedly while you were driving? It is as if that other driver were communicating to you that you were not worth paying attention to. You reacted in anger to the notion that someone could in effect be saying that to you.

In our idealistic ways of thinking, we would like to believe that it is possible to live life in complete harmony with one another. We think that if everyone would chip in and do his part there would be no such thing as separation between people. We would live together with no conflict. Though intellectually we know that this is impossible, emotionally we want to hold on to the idea. Anger is often simply a means of protecting ourselves from the painful reality of emotional separation.

Depression

Depression is nearly always an end result of a sense of isolation and separation from others. In fact, depression and loneliness are terms that are often used interchangeably to describe the same phenomenon. The person who suffers from depression is usually discouraged about himself and has a pessimistic outlook concerning the possibilities for happiness in his life.

The depressed person wants to be involved in a satisfying relationship with another person but has little hope of that occurring. He may think, "It's no use, it wouldn't work anyway; I'm no good." Or perhaps he thinks, "You can't depend on other people; no one is really what he seems to be." In other words, a depressed person tends to be either angry at himself or angry at other people or both. The anger is not always open or volatile, but it is there. It is simply subdued. The depressed individual's low mood is a reaction to the isolation he so desperately wants to avoid.

Depression arises when we become painfully aware that the perfect life we want is not to be found. When we refuse to accept some of the imperfections in our own life and in the world around us, we often retreat into this emotional state. Let us introduce you to someone who has experienced this problem.

Cynthia stated that her loneliness could best be described as deep hurt and depression. She was in her late thirties and was facing a painful and bitterly contested divorce. Her marriage of seventeen years had been rocky and unsettled all along. She had felt insecure on many occasions because of her husband's lack of devotion to her. But she had never known the depth of her fear of being emotionally isolated from her husband until he finally followed through on one of his numerous threats to file for divorce. The separation she had dreaded for years was finally a reality. In a way, she was relieved, but her basic reaction was hurt. She would spend hours, even days, in deep states of depression. Even though she knew that the marriage had not been solid, she had always held on to the hope that things might change. But hope existed no more. She was all alone.

Cynthia felt the intense sense of failure that so often comes with divorce. Her worth not only to other people but even to God seemed to have diminished. She wanted to blame her husband for the feelings she was experiencing, because, after all, it was his fault. In her heart she knew this was not so, but in her lowest moments it seemed to help to have someone to blame. Cynthia was feeling the full force of hurt and despair that she had so desperately tried to avoid in the previous years. Now she was left to suffer on her own.

Depression is built largely on a false assumption. The assumption is that when we are alone, life's value has diminished. Some people actually believe that when events do not happen as planned, there is absolutely no hope for a sense of contentment in their lives.

Do you see the interconnection between loneliness and depression? A sense of loneliness comes after one realizes there is a separateness between himself and another person (or sometimes between himself and God).

And depression follows when one is dissatisfied with that state of separateness and with himself.

A Sense of Rejection

Each of us has experienced rejection in one form or another. A child may have been rejected by playmates who did not like him. A teenager may feel rejected by his parents for not making high grades. A college senior may have been rejected in his attempts to be admitted to medical school. A marriage partner may have been rejected through divorce. The possibilities for feeling rejected are endless.

The feeling of rejection can have some severe emotional consequences. Loneliness and a sense of rejection go hand in hand. When we feel rejected, we are getting the message that we are not wanted. It is another reminder that human relationships are imperfect in that they do not always adequately fulfill our emotional needs. Rejection is not something to feel happy about, but neither does it have to be accompanied by overwhelming feelings of loneliness. Notice in the following example how rejection can so magnify a person's sense of loneliness that it can become destructive.

For Katherine, loneliness and rejection seemed to be one and the same. Katherine had known since she was a small child that her mother did not want her. She suspected that her mother had never wanted to become pregnant in the first place. She remembered clearly her mother's constant complaints that she was a pest and a nuisance. Katherine's father had left the family when she was very young because he did not want the hassle and responsibility of being a husband and a father. Katherine assumed that he left because he did not want her.

When Katherine was eighteen, she desperately wanted to leave home, so she got a job and moved into an apartment by herself. She was very intelligent, yet she had such little confidence in herself that she sought only menial work. She began to drift from one job to another because none of them proved to be very stimulating. This added further to her uncertainty and aimlessness. She would hang on to anyone who would give her the attention she craved. She would periodically have boyfriends, but they were never the type that would be sensitive to her emotional needs.

At the age of twenty-eight Katherine was still wandering from job to job, quite disillusioned with herself, with other people, and with God. What good is life when no one loves you? Her mother hated her, her father had left her, she made friends only out of sheer desperation. And to tell the truth, her friends were not really friends. They were just acquaintances who soon tired of her clinging. She assumed that even God rejected her because she did not see Him doing anything to make her life better. Everywhere she turned there was rejection. It became the norm. She expected nothing else.

There is a difference between the actual act of rejection and the feeling of rejection. The act of rejection occurs when we are given the message, either directly or subtly, that we are not wanted. The feeling of rejection goes a step further in that it is based on the assumption that we have been correctly deemed to be of little value. A person struggling with the feeling of rejection has allowed an unwanted and intolerable separation to lead him to the conclusion that he is worthless. Notice in the above example that Katherine was not only unable to live with the fact that she was not wanted (by some troubled people); she took it a step further by assuming that she was not lovable. She lost hope.

It is an unfortunate truth that each of us will be confronted by acts of rejection. When we are faced with rejection, we often mistakenly assume an "all-or-nothing" attitude: If people do not accept us all the way, we conclude we are worth nothing. In doing so, we are unnecessarily allowing the loneliness that is a part of our imperfect world to take up residency in our lives.

Anxiety

Anxiety is inappropriate fear and worry. It is a fear of the unknown. It is also a lack of faith. In trying to make light of anxiety, many people refer to it as concern. Concern refers to an appropriate interest in or regard for one's well-being or for another's circumstances. For example, when a child has health problems, parents will concern themselves. Anxiety, however, occurs when we allow ourselves to become overly concerned, or when we allow ourselves to become tense and worried over circumstances that do not logically warrant extreme emotions.

To say that a person can become completely free from anxiety would be a bit naive. A moderate amount of anxiety is normal. If you have ever spoken to a large group of people, you probably know what it is like to have a rapid heartbeat or a tightness in your stomach. Or perhaps you were tense as you awaited the outcome of a family member's surgery. Such situational anxiety is not necessarily harmful. However, if we live in a constant state of anxiety and tension, or if we let our worries debilitate us, our emotional stability is in danger.

So how does loneliness relate to anxiety? Let's examine what the emotion of anxiety communicates. When a person feels anxious, he is possibly communicating that he lacks confidence in himself or perhaps that he does not trust other people. Worse, anxiety may even be communicating that there is a lack of trust in God. The anxious person may be saying, "I am not 100 percent certain that my relationship with God is sufficient to help me through this situation"; or "I feel separated from others, and that disturbs me"; or "I am not completely comfortable with myself and my ability to handle things."

In other words, anxiety is a sense of uneasiness that grows from feeling uncomfortable with one's own imperfections, feeling out of step with people, or feeling out of touch with God. In a way, it is a fear of finding out the real or imagined truth about ourselves. Rather than taking active measures to remedy our situations (or accepting them), we channel our energies into worry. We allow ourselves to stew over the separations we experience in key relationships.

Will was a successful businessman in his mid-thirties. All of his life he had been performance-oriented. In fact, he considered himself an overachiever. In his climb up the ladder of success, he impressed many people and had offers to take on lucrative projects and business ventures. Consequently, Will found himself having to make formal business presentations to groups of colleagues. Unfortunately, Will had some insecurities that caused him to get very anxious whenever he had to make a presentation.

Since Will's chief goal was to impress people by his high achievements, he was excessively sensitive to the thought that people might find fault with him. He was constantly concerned that his public presentations would fail, so he worried about all the things that could go wrong. Subconsciously, he was afraid that if people did find fault with him, they would reject him, leaving him feeling lonely. His inappropriate fear was so great that he was living as if all of his negative prophecies were sure to come to pass.

Many people are very reluctant to accept the imperfect conditions in themselves or in other people. One woman had an accident that caused a finger to be slightly shortened. She became so worried that people would think less of her because of this that she stayed in a constant state of anxiety and depression. It was unbearable for her to think that people might have a reason to leave her alone.

Confusion

Many people experience times in their lives when confusion reigns. Times of confusion are characterized by disorderliness and a lack of clear direction. Confused persons feel disoriented, sometimes not knowing exactly what is going on in their life, or perhaps feeling helpless in their efforts to get a firm grip on their circumstances. There is a feeling of wandering about in a world of one's own while other people seem very distant, sometimes uncaring.

There is an obvious link between confusion and loneliness. We all experience times of uncertainty when we feel unable to come up with satisfactory answers to questions that arise in our lives. In interpersonal relationships this feeling comes to the fore when we feel insecure in our dealings with one another. There are times when, due to a sense of differentness and estrangement from others, we honestly do not know how to handle our behavior and emotions. When we feel securely linked and close to other people, confusion usually does not present much of a problem.

Chet was a seven-year-old boy who was brought to our clinic by his grandmother. His problem was that he did not seem to know how to interact with people. Sometimes he would withdraw from people for no known reason. At other times his behavior would be very inappropriate for the particular circumstances. When we took him into our play-therapy room for the first time, he simply stood in one place for the entire forty-five minutes, fidgeting with his fingers. He had been given permission to do whatever he wanted to do in the room, but he did not know what to do. (Most children would wander around and play with various toys.) Freedom was something he had never known.

For all of his short life, Chet had been a slave to circumstances. His mother was an unstable woman who kept changing her mind about whether to keep Chet at home with her or to let him live with his grandparents. Chet spent three or four years being shuttled back and forth from one home to another. He did not know where his loyalties should be. He did not know how to respond to a therapist who was willing to be his friend and let him make decisions for himself. He was so accustomed to feeling distant from other people that life was simply one big question mark.

Undoubtedly you have never been as confused as Chet. But there are times when each of us has a general sense of being disassociated from other people, causing us to feel incapable of handling personal and interpersonal problems. Confused people would like to be able to handle these problems, but they feel inadequate to the task.

Disillusionment

Disillusionment involves a feeling of bitterness when a person thinks he has been deceived or believes that the truth has been misrepresented to him. It is usually accompanied by a feeling that one's loyalties have been betrayed. Perhaps a person may enter a business deal on the sure advice of a friend, only to find out that it was not what it first appeared to be. Or perhaps a single person may have his hopes for marriage dashed when he finds that his loved one has been keeping secrets from him. Disillusionment is an uneasiness that a person experiences when he believes that a given circumstance should have turned out differently.

Many people will enter a relationship believing it to be something it is not. The cause for most divorces is that the marriage turned out to be less than what one or both marriage partners wanted, and accordingly was deemed unacceptable. Likewise, friendships can suffer serious setbacks when weaknesses or flaws that were not expected come to the surface. Some people go into retirement in hopes it will provide something it ultimately does not. And some people "put their trust in God" only to withdraw it when they find out they can't manipulate Him as they expected.

The possibilities for disillusionment are endless. Even though we do not want to accept the idea, there are in fact many flaws in ourselves and in others that cause relationships to change in ways we do not like. We like predictability. But sometimes our plans do not unfold as they are supposed to. Like the other emotions explored in this chapter, disillusionment is a reaction to the sense of loneliness that comes into our lives due to the imperfections around us.

Jim was a happy-go-lucky sort of fellow who seemed to get along well with most people. He was single, but he was planning to marry Lynn. That is, he thought that they would marry. A few months from the wedding date, Jim learned that Lynn had once had a sexual involvement with a former boyfriend. Jim had assumed she was sexually pure. When he asked her about this, she first denied it, but after relentless questioning she finally admitted that indeed it was true.

Jim immediately felt bitter because Lynn had not told him previously. Yet Lynn believed that since the experience was part of a very distant past there was no use in muddying the waters. She genuinely loved Jim and had made a full commitment to Christianity since then. But Jim kept going back to the fact that she had deceived him. He sensed there was a distance between them and felt very lonely when he was with her. Suddenly, Lynn was no longer the girl he expected her to be.

Each of us has entered situations only to learn that the facts are not as they once seemed. We have learned that many circumstances are not as ideal as we once hoped. Even though we know logically not to expect perfection, when imperfections arise we can sometimes be overwhelmed by the sense of isolation that results. For those who learn to accept or correct the imperfections, the disillusionment is short-lived. For those who find the imperfection too much to correct or accept, loneliness and disillusionment are inevitable.

The emotions that are interconnected with loneliness are too numerous to list. By studying how loneliness affects the emotions described in this chapter, we can learn how it affects other negative emotions as well. As we are able to overcome our feelings of loneliness, we will notice a marked change for the better in the other negative emotions in our lives.

PART 3

THE OVERCOMING OF LONELINESS

TEN

ENEMIES OF LONELINESS

IN THIS CHAPTER we will discuss six basic steps for overcoming loneliness. These general steps are some of the most powerful enemies of loneliness. In chapters 11 and 12 we will expand these six general steps into numerous specific steps for attaining emotional intimacy.

1. Be Active

Many people who are lonely passively sit around waiting for someone to come along or something to happen that will bring them out of their loneliness. They may misinterpret Isaiah 40:31, which states that they that wait on the Lord shall renew their strength. If we are feeling lonely, it helps to get up and do something—new activities, new interests, and meeting new people can all help. These suggestions are by no means a simplistic cure-all, but they really do help us break the cycle of loneliness and boredom. Yet it must be kept in mind that being active is but one small step. Many very active people are also very lonely deep within.

2. Unite with Other People

Lonely wives often improve significantly when their husbands begin spending more time communicating with them. In Ecclesiastes 4:11–12, Solomon notes: "Again, if two lie together, then they have heat: but how can one be warm alone? And if one prevail against him, two shall withstand him; and a threefold cord is not quickly broken" (KJV).

We recall a lonely woman who had been in and out of psychiatric institutions for years. Her pastor assigned two women in the church to meet with her each week for a year. That did more than any therapy had been able to do.

Of course, like our first suggestion, getting together with other people is inadequate by itself. An individual can be surrounded by people and still be lonely.

3. Have a Close Walk with God

A close walk with God is crucial. It is where the answer to loneliness starts. In 1 Samuel 30 we are told the story of David's returning home from battle to find that the women and children of his village had been taken captive by the enemy. David found himself in a very lonely position. Note the solution he found: "And David was greatly distressed; for the people spake of stoning him, because the soul of all the people was grieved, every man for his sons and for his daughters: but David encouraged himself in the LORD his God" (v. 6 KJV).

In John 16:32 Christ Himself stated, "Behold, the hour cometh, yea, is now come, that ye shall be scattered, every man to his own, and shall leave me alone; and yet I am not alone, because the Father is with me" (KJV).

We recall a lonely woman who had never known her father and whose mother had committed suicide. She found real comfort in Psalm 27:10: "For my father and my mother have forsaken me, but the LORD will take me up" (NASB). Truly, the most basic step in overcoming loneliness is a close walk with God through daily time spent with Christ. This will lead into the next step, which is . . .

4. Have the Fruits of the Spirit in Your Life

In Galatians 5:22–23 we read, "But the fruit of the Spirit is love, joy, peace, longsuffering, gentleness, goodness, faith, meekness, temperance: against such there is no law" (KJV). If we exhibit these fruits of the Spirit, others will want to be with us. Indeed, Solomon recorded that what is desirable in a man is kindness (Prov. 19:22). A critical and judgmental attitude, on the other hand, drives others away.

Not only does having the fruits of the Spirit in our life produce a positive attitude, but it also produces a sense of peace that will counteract loneliness. Furthermore, the indwelling Spirit gives us the ability to be patient and to forgive. We need to stop setting ourselves up to be lonely because of grudges we are holding against others. We are all depraved. We all fail at times. We have no right to hold grudges against those who fail us.

5. Realize the Love of Christ

Being grounded in love is probably the best cure for any emotional problem, including loneliness. The apostle Paul prayed "that Christ may dwell in your hearts by faith; that ye, being rooted and grounded in love, may be able to comprehend with all saints what is the breadth, and length, and depth, and height; and to know the love of Christ which passeth knowledge, that ye might be filled with all the fullness of God" (Eph. 3:17–19 KJV). Receiving the love that God imparts is vital if loneliness is to be cured, but giving love is also essential. Giving love usually results in receiving love.

6. Dwell on God's Promise That We Belong to Him

In order for a baby to grow up without inner loneliness he must feel that his parents will never forsake him and that he will always belong to them. Likewise, we as God's children need to continue to remind ourselves of the security we have in Him. Christ's promises are remarkably explicit:

> My sheep hear My voice, and I know them, and they follow Me; and I give eternal life to them, and they shall

> never perish; and no one shall snatch them out of My hand. My Father, who has given them to Me, is greater than all; and no one is able to snatch them out of the Father's hand. I and the Father are one.
>
> John 10:27–30 NASB

> Let not your heart be troubled; believe in God, believe also in Me. In My Father's house are many dwelling places; if it were not so, I would have told you; for I go to prepare a place for you. And if I go and prepare a place for you, I will come again, and receive you to Myself; that where I am, *there* you may be also.
>
> John 14:1–3 NASB

We are unconditionally loved and eternally secure in the hands of God if we have trusted Christ as our Savior.

ELEVEN

REALISTIC THINKING

HAVE YOU EVER BEEN OUT in the cold weather, shivering and wanting desperately to get indoors to the warmth? Do you recall the feeling when you finally stepped into a large, open room where there was a big stone fireplace that had a hot, blazing fire? It felt great, didn't it! Have you ever stopped to consider why that fire was so inviting and why it felt so good? The answer is simple. You had just experienced an uncomfortable coldness and chill. You knew that you couldn't stay cold indefinitely. Your body wanted and needed warmth, and you were able to appreciate the fire because it put an end to the discomfort of the cold. If you had not been so cold, the fire would not have been so welcome.

Such is the case when we find a way out of loneliness. There are times when each of us senses a separation from God and from other people. There are also times when we are disappointed in ourselves. Rather than allowing these experiences to drag us down in a feeling of defeat, we can find constructive ways both to get out of and to avoid falling into unhealthy patterns of living.

By accepting the truth that a measure of loneliness, or separateness, is natural for all people, it is possible to take some important steps toward developing a realistic philosophy of living. It is important for us to have a balanced, honest view of who we are. In this chapter we will examine several key teachings given to us in the Scriptures. These realistic thoughts and ideas will lead to a balanced style of living by helping us develop a philosophy that will allow us to recognize and *accept* that we are neither completely alone nor capable of being perfectly attached to another.

Sin Is a Part of Our Lives

The Bible teaches very clearly that we are all imperfect, falling short of God's original creation of mankind. "For all have sinned, and come short of the glory of God" (Rom. 3:23 KJV). "If we say that we have no sin, we deceive ourselves, and the truth is not in us" (1 John 1:8 KJV). In one of the most personal of his writings, Paul explains the workings of sin inside the individual:

> For that which I am doing, I do not understand; for I am not practicing what I would like to do, but I am doing the very thing I hate. . . . For I know that nothing good dwells in me, that is, in my flesh; for the wishing is present in me, but the doing of good is not. For

> the good that I wish, I do not do; but I practice the very evil that I do not wish.
>
> ROMANS 7:15, 18–19 NASB

Have you ever felt frustrations similar to those Paul was expressing? Sometimes you know beyond a shadow of a doubt that you should not do the very thing you are doing, but you do it anyway. There is no doubt that sin has a strong grip on each of us, just as it did with Paul. When we peer into our personalities, we find many flaws and weaknesses. We would like to pretend that sin is not so prominent in our lives, but we know better.

Now if life consisted of nothing more than this constant struggle with sin, we would be doomed to total misery. The person who focuses exclusively on his sin, advancing no further in self-awareness, is going to experience great troubles. In fact, the person who feels persistently lonely is usually keenly aware of the amount of imperfection in his life.

But fortunately Romans 7 does not leave us burdened with this struggle against sin:

> Wretched man that I am! Who will set me free from the body of this death? Thanks be to God through Jesus Christ our Lord! So then, on the one hand I myself with my mind am serving the law of God, but on the other, with my flesh the law of sin. There is therefore no condemnation for those who are in Christ Jesus.
>
> 7:24–8:1 NASB

Yes, it is true that sin plays an integral role in the way we live our lives. How sad that many people stop with the proclamation, "Wretched man that I am!" Fortunately, the Christian does not have to end with such a pessimistic conclusion.

God's Love Is Always Present

Sin and the resulting loneliness do not have to have the final say in our lives. While it is a fact that sin is present in each of us, it is also a fact that God loves us more than we can know. "For God so loved the world, that he gave his only begotten Son, that whosoever believeth in him should not perish, but have everlasting life" (John 3:16 KJV). "But God, being rich in mercy, because of His great love with which He loved us, even when we were dead in our transgressions, made us alive together with Christ (by grace you have been saved)" (Eph. 2:4–5 NASB).

Many people sadly are slow to recognize the immensity of the love of God. Our world is full of doubting Thomases. People try to make God's love too complicated. Some may feel that God could never love them because of the terrible wrongs they have committed. Others may think that God will start to love them when they perform more admirably. It is awesome to think that the love of God is given to us for *free*, no matter what type of imperfection exists within us.

A major reason that people are slow to comprehend the perfect love of God is that they are so accustomed to the imperfect ways in which humans love. All of us have at times felt that the love of another human is dependent on our meeting certain criteria. Are you familiar with this problem? Here are some examples: A person feels rejected by others because his skin is the wrong color; children may feel their parents love them only when they are good boys and girls; unless you belong to a certain type of church, you are not a real Christian.

Since human love is so often conditional, we assume that God's love and acceptance have conditions attached to them too. We need to keep in mind that while human love is imperfect and finite, God's love is perfect and infinite. We must not make assumptions about God's love based on the way people love.

Consider the following example of someone who struggled to understand the love of God. For all of his life, Philip had heard that God loved him. It was a fact that he simply accepted intellectually. But during a time of soul-searching, he began questioning just what that meant. He felt that he was too small for God to notice him, much less to love him. He began with the grim realization that he was only one of over four billion people on the face of the earth. One in four billion! That seemed fairly insignificant. Then Philip considered that in addition to all those people, God had billions upon billions of animals to watch over. Not only that, but there were the plants, the seas, the winds, and the rains for God to preside over. And all of this was demanding God's attention on just one planet! There were countless millions, maybe billions of stars in the universe. And, who knows, maybe there were other planets with other creatures demanding God's precious time. As Philip considered these thoughts, he felt small indeed. "Highly insignificant" might be more accurate. How could such a busy God ever have time to love just one person?

But in time, a different type of thought occurred to Philip. He remembered that on those occasions when he had felt the deepest personal needs God had *always* been there to guide him. Always! That meant that whenever he wanted and needed God's attention, God gave it. Out of all the billions of people on the earth and the trillions of countless creations in the universe, God would spend time with this one person. What love! What a feeling of excitement came over Philip! He had begun to grasp the fact that the Bible is indeed speaking to individuals when it says that God so loved the world.

This love, so immense, so far beyond our comprehension, is the key factor in each individual's search for a fulfilling life. The amazing part of it all is that God chooses to love each of us in spite of the fact that we are sinful.

Self-love Can Ease Lonely Feelings

We have a choice about the way we view ourselves. In laying a foundation for our particular style of life, we can focus primarily on the fact that we are sinful, or we can take refuge in the fact that God offers us lavish amounts of love. The wise choice is to focus on the idea that God willfully loves each of us. A view of self based on this truth can help us overcome trying experiences and lonely feelings.

This does not mean that we can simply dismiss sin as something irrelevant to our lives. Not at all. But it does mean that we can anchor ourselves in the hope offered to us through the love of God. Sin scars us and causes us to have experiences that are unpleasant and undesirable. Yet sin does not have to ruin our life. Remember, God's response to our sin is not to back away from us; He draws us even closer to Him in love because He knows of our deep need for Him.

There are plenty of reasons why many do not feel a love for themselves. Some people have been taught that the love of self is conceited or vain, representing a proud nature. Quite honestly, we have known some people who have proclaimed a love of self that, in truth, was vanity and pride. There are other people who clearly believe that their faults and hidden weaknesses make it impossible for them to simply decide to love themselves.

It may be easy enough for some people to intellectually recognize that they are loved by God, but when it comes to actually accepting that love in a very personal manner, they find it awkward. For others self-love just doesn't seem right. And still others abuse self-love by using it to blanket their sinful nature. Indeed it takes a specific style of thinking to know how to maintain an appropriate self-love.

The only absolute and certain foundation that we have to build our self-love upon is the unchanging character of God. We know that love is the chief characteristic of God's unchanging character:

> The one who does not love does not know God, for God is love.
>
> 1 JOHN 4:8 NASB

> Of old Thou didst form the earth;
> And the heavens are the works of Thy hands.
> Even they will perish, but Thou dost endure;
> And all of them will wear out like a garment;
> Like clothing Thou wilt change them, and they
> will be changed.
> But Thou art the same,
> And Thy years will not come to an end.
>
> PSALM 102:25–27 NASB

From the pages of Scripture we can also determine the extent of God's love: "But God demonstrates His own love toward us, in that while we were yet sinners, Christ died for us" (Rom. 5:8 NASB). It is mind-boggling to ponder the extent of the kind of love that is willing to sacrifice the life of a perfect Son.

For many of you God's unchanging love is not news. It may even be something you have heard all your life. Yet, if you experience uncomfortable bouts with loneliness, it is likely that your knowledge of God's love is not being put to work very well in your life. That is, you have not translated it into self-love. We may know volumes of information about the love of God and the love we can have for ourselves, but if that information does not work for us when we need it, something is missing.

By loving self, we are accepting the truth that God deems us lovable. We are recognizing that as one of God's own creations we can claim the worth that he places on each of us. Many people admit that it is easy enough to recognize that other people are part of God's creation and therefore worth loving. But it sometimes seems strange to feel that way toward ourselves. We must remind ourselves that self-love is not the same as pride and conceit. For those who develop an appropriate loving, caring attitude toward self, the fight against loneliness is well on the way to being won.

A Proper Perspective Is Essential

Seventy years here on earth is but a tiny drop when considered in the context of eternity. Our primary goal on earth is not to store up material goods or to become popular with other people. Rather, our chief aim in life is to develop a meaningful relationship with God through Jesus Christ and to help others do the same.

We often lose sight of this central goal in life. We mislead ourselves into pursuing selfish goals rather than keeping our eyes on the cross. Perhaps your number-one goal is to own a fine home, one that you can proudly show off to your friends. Or maybe your chief aim in life is to be loved and respected by your friends and acquaintances. Maybe you will feel satisfied only when your family life is in near-perfect order, giving you a sense of security and intimacy.

Do you suppose there is anything inherently wrong with any of the goals just mentioned? Of course not. It is natural to want to live in pleasant surroundings, to seek the love and respect of friends and acquaintances, and to desire fulfilling family relationships. However, if we come to worship the objects of these desires, we are not looking at life in proper perspective. We become slaves to wants and desires that are temporary in nature. Moreover, if these wants and desires are not satisfied, we will be plagued by disillusionment and loneliness. Now it is not wrong to desire to have some of the advantages in life. We simply must be certain to keep them in proper perspective.

So what does it mean to view life in proper perspective? It means that we are better off when we put first things first. We may pursue earthly goals, but only after we have accomplished the number-one goal in life, which is to seek after Christ. Notice how Scripture deals with this subject:

> Therefore I tell you, do not be anxious about your life, what you shall eat or what you shall drink, nor about

> your body, what you shall put on. Is not life more than food, and the body more than clothing? Look at the birds of the air: they neither sow nor reap nor gather into barns, and yet your heavenly Father feeds them. Are you not of more value than they? . . . But seek first his kingdom and his righteousness, and all these things shall be yours as well.
>
> MATTHEW 6:25–26, 33 RSV

In essence, Christ is here reminding His listeners that it is so easy to become bogged down with some of the everyday desires in life that we tend to lose sight of what is of supreme importance. By looking first to God and by seeking earnestly to know and experience His grace, and then putting it into action, we are assured that our every need in life will be met. This is a divine promise.

Think back to some time in your life when you felt especially lonely. It is very likely that at that time you were so keenly focused on the immediate problems in your life that you did not remember the promises given by God. If we are honest with ourselves, we will admit that it is quite easy to become so overwrought by our daily pressures that we lose proper perspective.

God Is Absolute—We Are Not!

God wants us to have a happy, fulfilling life. Even though we have faults and shortcomings, He does not want us to be swallowed up by the sense of loneliness they can bring. Nevertheless, many people allow themselves to be dominated by the pessimistic outlook on life that loneliness can bring. They will not feel content until everything in their lives is perfect.

Have you ever noticed how many people seem to have a black-and-white approach to living? We humans tend to think in terms of extremes, or absolutes. We are constantly making "either-or" judgments concerning events in our lives. Either our son will do well on his report card or he is in big trouble. Either my spouse will apologize for making that remark or I won't speak for the rest of the evening. Either I get that promotion or I'll quit.

Some of you may be thinking, "Maybe others are guilty of this, but not me." Think again. Do you ever catch yourself exaggerating with words such as "always" and "never"? "My wife is *always* late." "You *never* do nice things for me anymore." Or perhaps you overwork words such as "really." "This time I have *really* done it. I'll never get out of this mess."

So how does this relate to loneliness? Well, when things are not what we want them to be, we often lose sight of reality and begin to think in extreme terms. For example, when we feel somewhat discouraged, we may work ourselves up into thinking that our lives are completely hopeless and useless (a made-to-order setting for loneliness to take hold). We become quite skilled at taking a normal negative emotion and letting it get the best of us to the point of building an extreme, faulty lifestyle around it. Once we realize how inappropriate this extremism is, we can determine to take a more middle-of-the-road approach to life.

We need to recognize the balance offered to us in Scripture. It has already been pointed out that the Bible states quite clearly that we are sinful and imperfect. That should be enough to keep us from becoming egotistical.

But we have also discussed how God sees us as lovable creations of high worth. This truth can keep us from plunging down to extreme negative thinking.

Keep in mind an amazing fact about the Bible. While it sets before us commandments and directives for the ideal way of living, there is also an inherent understanding that we are struggling with sin. Consequently, God is gracious toward us while He patiently and lovingly exhorts us to leave our worldly ways behind. Consider, for example, Romans 5:18–21:

> Then as one man's [Adam's] trespass led to condemnation for all men, so one man's [Jesus'] act of righteousness leads to acquittal and life for all men. For as by one man's disobedience many were made sinners, so by one man's obedience many will be made righteous. Law came in, to increase the trespass; but where sin increased, *grace abounded all the more*, so that, as sin reigned in death, grace also might reign through righteousness to eternal life through Jesus Christ our Lord. (RSV, italics added)

While Adam, representing all people, fell into sin, Christ lived the perfect life of righteousness. Because of Him, we are not doomed to negative extremes. Because of God's love for us, our life, though sinful, can begin to approach that of the Savior. This is not of our own doing but is purely of God's grace.

Only when Christians realize that we do not fit into either extreme (we are neither all good nor all bad) can we gain control over our emotions. You see, emotions often are not very smart. That is, emotions often do not slow down long enough to view life from a balanced perspective. It is easy for our emotions to go to the extreme.

While God's nature is perfect and unwavering, ours is not. We are up and down. God is absolute. To believe that our lives should also be absolute goes against biblical teachings about humanness.

To some of you, this information is new. But to others, this information is very familiar. Yet there are many Christians who know the facts about sin and grace but live in misery and emotional turmoil. Why is this? The answer is simple. People who have a knowledge of God's grace but continue to live topsy-turvy emotional lives have not translated this knowledge into their hearts through faith. They still regard their lives in terms of extremes.

Faith Is the Necessary Glue

Having an intellectual belief about something may make very little difference in our lives. This is where faith steps in. Look at the definition of faith: "Now faith is the assurance of things hoped for, the conviction of things not seen" (Heb. 11:1 RSV). When the Bible refers to faith as the ingredient that gives us assurance, it is saying that faith is the basis on which our belief system stands. Faith gives substance to our hopes and beliefs.

Perhaps you are like a young man we counseled who insisted that he believed in God and would gladly live his life for God if He would only make His presence known to him in a physical way. The young man's problem was that he was not allowing his belief in God to take substantive root in his life. Simply put, he lacked faith.

You may ask, "Well, why do we have to have faith in things unseen in the first place? If God is almighty, why doesn't He just come down from heaven and live right here with us? That would eliminate all the mystery of the unseen things." The problem is that He already has lived among us here on earth—in the person of Jesus Christ! And amazingly, the majority of the people hated and rejected Him. So even though God's message of victory over life's imperfections has been presented in a clear-cut manner, faith is important in order to quiet our skeptical minds. Without it we lack spiritual perception. With it we can in some measure comprehend what God has done and will do for us.

Faith brings our belief in God down from a merely intellectual level to a very personal one. By faith we not only believe in the promises of God, but we also feel in our hearts that they are true. It is, of course, correct to start with the proper beliefs; faith then takes us one step further by adding the glue that makes those beliefs a part of our entire lifestyle.

Randy was a man in his late thirties who had some specific beliefs about God, but his beliefs did not seem to help much. He was depressed and unhappy much of the time. He called himself a Christian, but in truth, he did not fully know what that meant. He assumed that since he knew *about* Christ, he was a Christian. As his low feelings persisted, he was about to conclude that Christianity was not pertinent to his personal needs.

As Randy shared his thoughts with us, it became apparent that he had not translated his intellectual knowledge into a belief system that was based on faith. When the Bible says that we must believe in the Lord Jesus Christ in order to be saved (Acts 16:31), it does not mean that we are simply to accumulate facts about Him. It means that we are to trust that God has saved us from our wretchedness through Christ's death on the cross and His resurrection.

All too often people fail to apply such faith to their system of intellectual thoughts. Many boys and girls put together model airplanes. They may know exactly where each piece of the model fits, but such knowledge makes no material difference until they apply the glue. In our spiritual lives, faith is the glue. We may know many facts about Christianity and how it is supposed to direct our lives, but our knowledge will be of little consequence until we couple it with a deep faith in Christ.

TWELVE

DO SOMETHING ABOUT IT!

IN THIS CHAPTER we are going to look at how we can make our beliefs come alive by *doing* something with them. It is natural once we have a solid belief system to go out and put it into *action:* "But be doers of the word, and not hearers only, deceiving yourselves" (James 1:22 RSV). "What does it profit, my brethren, if a man says he has faith but has not works? . . . So faith by itself, if it has no works, is dead" (James 2:14, 17 RSV). "He who says he abides in him ought to walk in the same way in which he walked" (1 John 2:6 RSV). We may have a superb belief system regarding God, but if it is not combined with action it will result only in disappointment.

We have seen that while God has given us a victory over sin through Jesus Christ, sin is still present in our lives and can cause emotional scars. We will continue to be bothered by the effects of sin unless we take active steps away from it. That is why we are commanded in the Bible to do what is right. God, in His infinite love and wisdom, knows that we need prodding in order to keep ourselves from following our naturally selfish nature.

Unfortunately, some people expect emotional stability and happiness simply to fall into their laps as a result of their profession of Christianity. They think, "I am a Christian, so why don't I feel good? What's wrong with God; has He forgotten me?" No, God never forgets us. But He wants us to put some effort into our Christian lives. He wants us to work at achieving happiness. He knows that we are more committed to something when we choose to work for it. God invites us to be *partners* in the cleansing process. Make no mistake: God is the major partner, but we need to make our contributions too.

This chapter presents various suggestions for us to take to heart in our struggle to overcome loneliness. God has made it possible for us to overcome our negative feelings; it is up to us to complete the task with our efforts.

Make Life a Growing Process

Many people have difficulty with Matthew 5:48, where Christ says to His listeners, "You, therefore, must be perfect, as your heavenly Father is perfect." But can a person who is prone to sin even dream of being perfect? That seems impossible. But there it is in black and white in the Bible.

What is Christ trying to say to us in these few words? Biblical scholars have suggested that a more accurate translation of the Greek word *teleios* (translated "perfect") would be "maturing." Now reread the verse with this different translation in mind. Does the goal seem more attainable? When Jesus exhorts His followers to mature, He is not laying down some new law that must be very strictly enforced by the church leaders. Rather, He is implying that He has set the perfect human example, and if we are earnest in our desire to follow Him, we will emulate that example.

Consider the case of a young man who is just starting out in the carpentry business. At first he will be in constant need of instruction and supervision. As he continues in the learning process, he will acquire some of the finer skills of the trade; as time goes by, a knowledgeable observer will be able to see marked improvement in his craft. However, the young carpenter will never reach a point at which everything he produces is perfect. There will always be room for refinement. There may even be periods when he appears to be in a professional slump. But on the whole his work will continue to improve and mature.

Just as any tradesman wants to improve his handiwork, we will want to continue to grow spiritually. Certainly there will be times when we feel we are going backward (e.g., periods of loneliness). But we will commit ourselves to do whatever we can to keep a forward progression in our lives. Thus, at times we will be taking two steps forward and one step backward. That is to say, there may be setbacks, but the overall movement will be forward.

The Bible has an apt illustration of what can happen to a person when he fails to move forward. It is the story of Jonah. Jonah was called by God to speak before the people of the city of Nineveh to warn them of the wrath of God unless they repented of their sins. Though Jonah tried to run away from God's calling, he eventually (after a series of adventures) made his way to Nineveh to do what God had asked him to do.

Much to Jonah's surprise, when he preached to the townspeople they actually listened to him and repented. From pauper to king they determined to give up their wickedness and turn to God. Do you remember what Jonah's reaction was to all of this? He pouted! And then he became depressed and lonely. Jonah had believed that God was merciful only to the people of his own nation. When he saw God bestow His grace on these foreigners, he was angry.

Imagine being angry because a whole city had decided to follow God! It is quite obvious that Jonah was not trying to mature in his relationship with God. He serves as a good illustration that when a person does not progress, he is likely going to regress. Humans rarely stagnate. The story of Jonah demonstrates that if we fail to accept and rejoice in the gifts of God, we are doomed to a life of recurring loneliness and depression.

Live One Day at a Time

There are two things that occupy people's minds too much—the past and the future. Many people who are suffering from loneliness are trying to live more than one day at a time. They are trying to live yesterday, today, and tomorrow all at the same time.

There are those who constantly live in the past, rehashing old mistakes, saying to themselves, "If only I could have . . ." All of us have made errors in judgment that we would like to correct. And all of us have in some way or another had to pay the consequences of past wrongdoings. Certainly one of the reasons God gave us a memory was to remind us of our mistakes, so we would not commit them again. However, all too often people become so deeply entrenched in their past that they are riddled by pessimism and a sense of doom.

We cannot begin to count the times that we have sat in our counseling offices with people whose shame over the past is like a millstone tied around their necks. Because of their past they feel as though there is no help for the future. As a result, they become increasingly pessimistic and eventually conclude that their life is worth very little. Regarding themselves as losers, they expect to be failures and therefore create one failure after another in their lives.

Live one day at a time. Learn to put the mistakes of the past behind you—except to learn from them. Drop your grudges and learn to forgive. Give up your negativism and learn to find the bright side of life. (There is one, you know.)

The apostle Paul wrote, "For I have learned, in whatever state I am, to be content" (Phil. 4:11 RSV). He was teaching his readers to make the best of what they have at the present time. (Amazingly, Paul was locked in prison at the time he wrote those words.) He had learned to live in a present-tense state of contentment in spite of his past. Before he became a Christian, he had been a coldhearted man, a murderer. Consider his reminiscences when he appeared before Agrippa:

> My manner of life from my youth, spent from the beginning among my own nation and at Jerusalem, is known by all the Jews. . . . I myself was convinced that I ought

> to do many things in opposing the name of Jesus of Nazareth. And I did so in Jerusalem; I not only shut up many of the saints in prison, by authority from the chief priests, but when they were put to death I cast my vote against them. And I punished them often in all the synagogues and tried to make them blaspheme; and in raging fury against them, I persecuted them even to foreign cities.
>
> ACTS 26:4, 9–11 RSV

Paul readily admitted that he had a shameful past. Today, many can make the same admission. Many people look at their past and recall that they were sexually promiscuous, or that they abused their bodies with drugs or alcohol, or perhaps that they placed family life too low on their list of priorities. Whatever our past, we all can find some good reason to hang our heads in shame. But living in the past, dwelling on the negatives, is simply uncalled for.

Notice how Paul handled this potential problem. In referring to his personal history, he wrote, "I have been crucified with Christ; it is no longer I who live, but Christ who lives in me" (Gal. 2:20 RSV). "But one thing I do, *forgetting what lies behind* and straining forward to what lies ahead, I press on toward the goal for the prize of the upward call of God in Christ Jesus" (Phil. 3:13–14 RSV, italics added). Yes, Paul had quite a past, a wretched one, one that surely was unpleasant to recall. But he came to the conclusion that he would never be able to live an effective life until he was able to put it well behind him.

Not only are people burdened by the past, but many are quite skilled at living in the future. They constantly ask themselves, "What will I do if this or that happens?"

worrying about something they have no control over. What a headache it can be to feel that we have to settle the problems of the future today. "If only I could get the salary increase I need, life would be tolerable." "When the man of my dreams comes along, I know I will finally be happy."

Each hour we spend focusing on the future means that we will have that much less time to live for the present. This is not to say that we should never plan for the future. But there is no point to wasting energy on wishing and dreaming about the future when we can use that same energy to make the present a better time and place to live.

The psalmist wrote, "This is the day which the LORD has made; let us rejoice and be glad in it" (Ps. 118:24 RSV). There is no need to burden ourselves with grief from the past, nor is it necessary to create new burdens with worries concerning the future. We have all that we can handle in just living for today.

Have an Understanding for Other People

One of the reasons people experience loneliness is that they push others away instead of trying to understand them. Learning to understand others can go a long way toward bridging the gaps that exist between us. Keep in mind, understanding is something you *give* away; it is a gift. As we concentrate more on what we give other people, we will not have to be concerned about what we receive. Giving is contagious. It usually causes the recipient to want to give in return. Even if the recipient is not giving in return, you still have lost nothing but have gained much.

Key to an understanding attitude is the development of empathy. Empathy is the ability to readily comprehend, almost to feel as it were, another person's emotions and attitudes. Or as the proverb has put it, it is the ability to walk a mile in the other person's moccasins. Often in our desperate desire for others to understand our feelings, we forget to return the favor. By seeking to understand others, there is less tendency to focus on the minor problems in our own lives.

Now the ability to empathize will get a person nowhere if it is not put to use. It really does not take much skill to be able to discover another person's feelings. For example, a glum look or unusual silence enables us to detect when someone is sad. Being empathic involves more: It includes *communicating* your understanding of another person's experiences to that person.

Communicating to another person that you understand his feelings is not all that difficult. For example, when a person looks sad, you might simply say, "You look quite discouraged right now," or, "That really got you down." You may not know exactly how to pull him out of his negative feelings, but by demonstrating understanding, you can help him to make a start. You can use your concern to draw yourself toward other people. You may not always condone another person's feelings or attitudes, but you can at least try to see things from his point of view.

Do you know what the normal human reaction is when other people express their feelings? Instead of showing understanding we try to tell them what to do with their feelings. For example, have you ever told someone, "Don't be discouraged; everything will be all right"? Or, "Why don't you ease up on your anger; it's not doing any good"? These types of statements show a condescending attitude on your part. It is as if you are convinced that you know what the other person should do and that he is incapable of figuring out how to live his life.

You might be surprised at what an understanding attitude can do to help ease someone else's negative feelings. For that matter, an understanding attitude can bolster another's positive feelings. Moreover, you will probably find that as you increase your level of empathy, you will be less likely to feel lonely. The key quality of empathy is that it draws people together.

Accept Imperfections in Others

Have you ever wondered what causes people to have a critical nature? It is caused in part by an unaccepting attitude toward people. One can readily see how this can cause a person to slip into periods of loneliness. In fact, a circular pattern develops: When people feel lonely, they tend toward criticism of others, which perpetuates loneliness, which . . .

Many people seem to believe that it will be easier to accept themselves if they are able to find unacceptable traits in others. (Misery loves company.) But the person battling loneliness defeats himself if he has a critical or unaccepting nature. It would be helpful for him instead to accept that others will be imperfect, recognizing that it is futile to expect perfection from them. Nor is there any need to gloat over another person or to feel superior. (Doing this is actually a sign that we feel inferior.)

While there may be some people who have particularly distasteful habits, a balanced view of life recognizes that in every person there is something worthwhile. This means that people can be accepted in spite of negative characteristics. The critical, nonaccepting attitude is the opposite of the love God expects us to give: "If any one says, 'I love God,' and hates his brother, he is a liar; for he who does not love his brother whom he has seen, cannot love God whom he has not seen. And this commandment we have from him, that he who loves God should love his brother also" (1 John 4:20–21 RSV).

It is wise to remember the old adage, "There but for the grace of God go I," whenever we feel unaccepting toward someone. Because of human nature, all men are prone to sin and improper conduct. Yet, because of the grace of God, some of us have learned more appropriate behavior than have others. (Don't get fooled into thinking you are superior to anyone.) In and of ourselves we are no better or worse than anyone else. We are simply different from one another.

As an illustration of this point, consider the case of a man who spent his life working with convicted felons in prison settings. He dealt with the full range of criminals—from the smalltime car thief to murderers on death row. Given the common social attitudes toward prison inmates, it would have been easy for him to develop an unaccepting attitude toward the people he dealt with. But there seemed to be one humbling thought that always stayed with him. He wondered how he would have turned out if his parents have been like the parents of some of the criminals, if he had grown up in their neighborhoods, if he had rubbed shoulders with the same people. His conclusion was always the same. He felt he probably would have become a criminal. He knew himself well enough to admit that he was very capable of being imperfect. And given the right (or rather, wrong) set of circumstances, that side of him could easily have become dominant. As a result of this admission to himself, it was difficult for him to assume an unaccepting attitude toward the prisoners. Consequently, he was able to make friends with people who by society's standards were considered unfit. He knew that "there but for the grace of God go I."

In theory, this accepting attitude is easy for all of us to endorse. But when it comes to some of our close relationships, it can be easily forgotten. For example, have you ever noticed that you might become provoked with a family member over some behavior that you might accept in someone else? It is common to find that people will criticize their spouse or children more severely than they would their friends or business associates. It is relatively easy to accept the faults of a person you do not live with. The true test is whether you are able to accept the same faults in those closest to you, namely, family members.

An accepting attitude goes a long way toward overcoming loneliness. Like understanding, it can be a form of giving. An accepting attitude will work toward closing the gaps that exist in your relationships and will help build unity.

Learn to Be Forgiving

An unforgiving spirit and an unwillingness to forget can be sure contributors to loneliness. Unfortunately, there are too many people who focus on the negative side of life, becoming experts at holding grudges and keeping others at a distance. It is obvious that such an attitude will contribute to lonely feelings.

Christ gave us a very specific teaching regarding forgiveness: "Then Peter came up and said to him, 'Lord, how often shall my brother sin against me, and I forgive him? As many as seven times?' Jesus said to him, 'I do not say to you seven times, but seventy times seven'" (Matt. 18:21–22 RSV). Actually, when Peter asked Jesus this question, he was somewhat proud of himself. For in those days, it was the rabbinic teaching that a man must forgive his brother seven times. Certainly Peter expected to be commended by Jesus. But Jesus' answer was a surprise. He said we are to forgive our brother seventy times seven, or an unlimited number of times. There is no limit to forgiveness. Jesus exemplified this principle as He was dying on the cross: "And Jesus said, 'Father, forgive them; for they know not what they do'" (Luke 23:34 RSV). Even when mankind was committing its gravest sin, Christ was willing to forgive.

Christ, of course, is the perfect model of forgiveness. He says to us, "I accept you and love you in spite of your continued shortcomings. Just ask, and forgiveness is yours—free." A failure to forgive indicates that there is a flaw in our ability to love. If we truly desire to build bridges in our relationships, we will be willing to forgive time and time again.

Share Your Burdens with Someone

One reason people struggle with loneliness is that they keep their feelings and problems bottled up inside, never sharing them with anyone. We are not encouraging you to tell your problems to the nearest television reporter for broadcast on the nightly news. But we are suggesting that you will not feel quite so overwhelmed if you know you have an ally giving you support.

The Scriptures indicate that we should have a sense of teamwork when there are problems to be solved: "Bear one another's burdens, and so fulfil the law of Christ" (Gal. 6:2 RSV). Our lives here on earth were never meant to be spent in solitude. The Bible recognizes that people can be useful simply by listening to one another's problems. Many times counselees leave our offices with a tremendous sense of relief simply because they know that someone is trying to understand.

People will often give the excuse that their problems are too great or too embarrassing to be shared with anyone. And some of them truly have had wild experiences. But no matter how wild or how embarrassing our problems, we are only adding to our misery if we never share ourselves with someone. Certainly we will want to be discreet in choosing how we will share our feelings and with whom we will share them. Sometimes it is best to talk with a professional counselor or a minister we can trust.

Mark was a man in his mid-thirties who came to our clinic recently to discuss problems that he described as depression and insecurity. He had never seen a counselor before, nor had he ever talked about his problems with anyone. He began sharing some of his deepest emotions. He felt that he had been rejected all his life, that he was never good enough for anyone to like him. He had never shared his feelings with his wife and children for fear they would think he was crazy. As a result, there was a growing sense of detachment from them.

Mark talked on and on about several of his personal insecurities, weaknesses that really bothered him. It was obvious that he was aching for someone to understand him, flaws and all. As the first session drew to a close, he remarked that the counselor probably would not like him very much after learning of his weaknesses. When he was assured that that was not the case, that the counselor intended to work very closely with him to help him learn to appreciate himself, a deep sigh of relief came out: "Why didn't I do something like this fifteen years ago when it all got started?"

After further sessions, Mark became more comfortable about sharing his feelings. He found out that he was able to open up to his wife; much to his surprise he discovered that she had experienced similar feelings. By coming out in the open with his feelings, Mark learned that he was not as alone as he had once assumed.

Develop an Active Prayer Life

Sometimes a lonely person who seeks help from a friend or a minister gets the answer: "Well, you just need to pray about your problems and the Lord will work them out." This advice can rub many people the wrong way. Too often it is given in an unsympathetic manner. But let's not be so critical of this response that we overlook it altogether.

Prayer can be an extremely effective tool in overcoming loneliness. In 1 Thessalonians 5:17 we are given the simple directive: "Pray without ceasing." Now of course, this verse is not saying that we must always be on our knees in prayer toward God. That would be impossible. But it is encouraging us to be in a constant *state* of prayer. That is, all of our actions are to be conducted as unto God. All of our conversations are to be spoken as with God. We are to be in a constant state of awareness that we are in God's presence. There is to be a constant state of reverence and humbleness in our daily living.

This does not mean that we are to live boring, stuffy lives, constantly steeped in deep thought. There are many "religious" people like this, and they lead fairly dull lives. Some people are so heavenly minded that they are no earthly good. What "pray without ceasing" does mean is that we are to be in a constant state of awareness and appreciation of our God. The more we allow ourselves to sense God's constant presence in our lives, the more willing and able we will be to involve ourselves in meaningful tasks.

To "pray without ceasing" also means that our line of communication with God is consistently open. He is there when we want to give Him thanks or praise. He is there when we need to share our feelings with someone. He is there when we have requests to make. He will be a constant part of our lives if only we allow Him to be.

As we allow ourselves to enter this constant state of prayer, our level of commitment to other Christian pursuits will increase. A life centered around Christian activities is going to be happier and less prone to loneliness.

Prayer is a privilege we have been given by God. And even when we do not have adequate words to express our thoughts, we can still pray. The Holy Spirit, knowing our innermost thoughts, is able to intercede for us: "Likewise the Spirit helps us in our weakness; for we do not know how to pray as we ought, but the Spirit himself intercedes for us with sighs too deep for words"

(Rom. 8:26 RSV). God desires so much to be in constant communication with us that He has sent us His Holy Spirit to assist us. This is another indication of His desire to be close to us. We are told: "Draw near to God and he will draw near to you" (James 4:8 RSV).

Christians can use prayer as a means to draw close to God and stay close. Non-Christians can use prayer to invite Jesus Christ into their lives so they, too, can have constant communion and companionship with Him.

Never Give Up on Yourself

There is much wisdom to the old saying, "If at first you don't succeed, try, try again." By applying this saying to the problem of loneliness, we can motivate ourselves to put a positive plan of life into action. We are given the promise: "No temptation has overtaken you that is not common to man. God is faithful, and he will not let you be tempted beyond your strength, but with the temptation will also provide the way of escape, that you may be able to endure it" (1 Cor. 10:13 RSV). Though we may be tempted to give in to the feeling of loneliness, we know that there are ways to overcome it.

Become Aware of Your Loneliness

One of the primary aims of this book is to help increase your awareness of the reasons for and consequences of loneliness. But we all know through simple logic that awareness of a problem is useless in and of itself. Knowledge of a problem must be used to help solve that problem. In our counseling sessions, we often encourage people to become "outside observers," watching their own behavior and listening to their own thoughts. We want their degree of self-awareness to be at such a level that their intellectual understanding of their problems will give them the motivation to change.

After several days of self-observation, many people are surprised at the extent of loneliness that exists in their lives. Some of them prefer to deny their loneliness by calling it depression, sadness, or apathy. But the fact is that as we become aware and admit that loneliness is at the base of many other personal problems, we also become better equipped to make constructive changes in our lives.

You may question, "If I become more aware of my loneliness, won't it just make me feel worse?" It can. But it does not have to. When a baseball player becomes aware of a flaw in his batting swing, he feels bad about it at first, but then he is able to correct it and improve his game. Such is the case when we become aware of the fact that human nature makes us prone to feel lonely. We can make this awareness work for us, not against us.

A minister friend of ours tells of a personal experience that opened his eyes to a sense of smugness that caused him to experience loneliness. Early in his ministry, he had the opportunity to visit a small island off the coast of Central America. An ancient Indian tribe of about fifteen hundred people inhabited the island. The purpose of this journey was to consult with a man who had grown up on the island and was now serving as a missionary there. As our friend stepped off the boat, he immediately noticed that there were no streets or sidewalks. There was no evidence that the island had been touched by modern civilization. Most of the dwelling places were small huts with thatched roofs. This was quite a difference for a man who lived in a comfortable, air-conditioned home in a suburban neighborhood.

As our friend was being escorted to his quarters, he was told that his host had one of the finest homes on the island, so his spirits were lifted a bit. Rather than having a thatched roof, this home was made of adobe and was fairly solid. Nonetheless, it was still quite primitive by the minister's standards. There was an open doorway leading into the house, but no door. There were window openings, but no window panes or coverings. There was one bedroom where all of the family members would roll out their mats and sleep together. Of course there was no plumbing, so water had to be carried from a stream several hundred yards away. The minister had an uneasy feeling about spending several nights in such a place. Before he came to the island he knew he would not be staying at a luxury hotel. But he hadn't expected quite so primitive a situation. His thoughts began to be negative, and his heart was no longer in his mission.

By late afternoon, our minister friend was hungry, and he was looking forward to a good meal. Being the guest of honor, he knew that he would be treated to a special meal; and indeed he was. But what the Indians considered to be special was far from being grand in the minister's opinion. He was served a modest bowl of rice and pork gravy with a little coconut sprinkled on top. Much to his disappointment, that was the entire meal. While his host family was delighted by such a fine meal, he was feeling disappointed because it seemed barely sufficient for his dietary needs.

After the meal was completed, the host family had a special time of prayer and thanksgiving. The Indian father began by thanking God for the beautiful ocean that literally surrounded their home. He thanked God for the shade trees and the coconuts, for the wind and the smell of the ocean breeze, for their more than adequate home and their bounteous material blessings, for his health and his family's health. He went on and on thanking God for so many of these gifts of nature that a lump came to the minister's throat and he found himself brushing back the tears that stained his cheeks.

Before the prayer the minister had not allowed himself to experience and enjoy the bounteous blessings bestowed on the people of this tiny remote island. Primitive as their lifestyle was, these people had a deep sense of appreciation for their position in God's universe. Their desire for material possessions seemed so small that the minister was embarrassed that he had thought of them as a group of underprivileged people. During his week-long stay on the island, he came to learn that these people actually had a better knowledge and appreciation of God's goodness because they were not hampered by burdening thoughts and ideas about what satisfied living is.

Had not our friend's eyes been opened to his misconceptions and inappropriate attitudes, he would have found himself plunged into loneliness and frustration. The prayer of the Indian father caused the minister to become acutely aware of his improper thoughts and feelings. Only after he became aware of the inappropriateness of his response to the island people was he able to correct himself.

As we set out with the task of overcoming feelings of loneliness, we need to be honest with ourselves in determining our flaws that lead to loneliness. Once we become aware of what is going on inside ourselves, we have a starting place to work from. Awareness is the first step.

You may wonder, "If we can actually grow as a result of our awareness of flaws within ourselves, why do so many people react so negatively when their flaws are identified?" The answer lies in the manner in which they accept their flaws. A well-adjusted person will not be overwhelmed by an awareness of his personal defects. He will realistically and rationally take into account that it is normal for each of us to have both strengths and weaknesses.

On the other hand, there are people who hate to admit that they have any weaknesses. Also, there are people who become distraught when yet another weakness is exposed—perhaps their list of weaknesses seems unending, causing discouragement. Consequently, we find that there are many people, for whatever reasons, who are afraid to look at their own faults. They will likely suffer repeatedly the effects of loneliness because they refuse to confront the problem head on.

Practice Mature Communication with Your Mate

Mature communication of our feelings is one of the most important steps for building intimacy in marriage (as well as in all other relationships). Even the proper sharing of negative emotions such as anger builds intimacy. Burying negative emotions inside ourselves results only in increased distances, depression, and loneliness. We give here twenty-four "Guidelines for Fighting Fair in Marriage"[1] and encourage you to put them into practice diligently:

1. Sincerely commit your lives to Jesus Christ as Lord.
2. Consider marriage a lifelong commitment, just as Christ is eternally committed to His bride, the church.
3. Agree to always listen to each other's feelings, even if you consider your mate's feelings to be inappropriate.
4. Commit yourselves to both honesty and acceptance.
5. Determine to attempt to love each other *unconditionally*, with each partner assuming 100 percent of the responsibility for resolving marital conflicts (the 50/50 concept seldom works).
6. Consider all the factors in a conflict before bringing it up with your mate.
7. Confess any personal sin in the conflict to Christ before confronting your mate.
8. Limit the conflict to the here and now—*never bring up past failures,* since all past failures should already have been forgiven.
9. Eliminate the following phrases from your vocabulary:
    "You never" and "You always."
    "I can't" (what you really mean is, "I won't").
    "I'll try" (this usually means, "I'll make a halfhearted effort but won't quite succeed").
    "You should" and "You shouldn't." (these are parent-to-child statements).
10. Limit the discussion to the one issue that is the center of the conflict.
11. Focus on that issue rather than attacking each other.

12. Ask your mate if he would like some time to think about the conflict before discussing it (but never put discussion off past bedtime—see Eph. 4:26).
13. Each mate should use "I feel . . ." messages, expressing his response to whatever words or behavior aroused the conflict. For example, "*I feel* angry toward you for coming home late for supper without calling me first" is an adult-to-adult message, whereas, "*You should* always call me when you're going to be late for supper" is a parent-to-child message. A parent-to-child message will cause the mate to become defensive.
14. Never say anything derogatory about your mate's personality. Proverbs 11:12 tells us that "he who despises [belittles] his neighbor lacks sense" (NASB).
15. Even though your mate won't always be correct, consider your mate an instrument of God working in your life. Proverbs 12:1 says, "He who hates reproof is stupid" (NASB).
16. Never counterattack, even if your mate does not follow these guidelines.
17. Don't tell your mate why you think he does what he does (unless he asks you), but rather stick to how you feel about what he does.
18. Don't try to read your mate's mind. If you're not sure what he meant by something he said, ask him to clarify it.
19. Learn to deal with your anger biblically.[2]
    a. Gain insight into whether your anger is appropriate or inappropriate.
    b. Verbalize your appropriate anger and forgive before bedtime.

   c. Never try to get vengeance—leave that to God.
20. Be honest about your emotions, but keep them under control. Proverbs 29:11 says, "A fool always loses his temper, but a wise man holds it back" (NASB). Proverbs 15:18 says, "A hot-tempered man stirs up strife, but the slow to anger pacifies contention" (NASB).
21. Remember that resolution of the conflict is what is important, not who wins or loses. If the conflict is resolved, you both win. You're on the same team, not opposing teams.
22. Agree with each other on what topics are out of bounds because they are too hurtful or have already been discussed (e.g., in-laws or continued obesity).
23. Pray about each conflict before discussing it with your mate.
24. Commit yourselves to carefully learn and practice these guidelines for "fighting fair" in marriage and agree with each other to call "foul" whenever one of you accidentally or purposefully breaks one of these guidelines. (You may even choose to agree on a dollar fine for each violation!)

THIRTEEN

LEARNING FROM BIBLICAL CHARACTERS

WHEN SOMEONE FEELS LONELY and discouraged, it is common for him to assume that he is the only one in the world who knows what it is like to suffer. And inasmuch as one of the consequences of loneliness is a feeling of inferiority, the lonely person also assumes that others are much better equipped to fend off lonely feelings. We forget that even the greatest of men and women have their low moments too.

While we each have different personalities and differing styles of handling conflict, we need to keep in mind that all of us are subject to human frailties. One way to keep things in perspective is to look at the lives of some great people in biblical times. In the brief character sketches that follow, we will be focusing primarily on their feelings of loneliness. We have the advantage of hindsight, which means that as we psychoanalyze their lives, we can learn from their experiences. As we read about these individuals, we may find parallels between their lives and our own. We will find that even though they are thought of as great heroes of faith, they are very similar to us.

Joseph

Interpersonal conflicts often result in loneliness. The story of Joseph is a prime example of interpersonal conflicts that could have resulted in loneliness if Joseph had not had a proper attitude. His brothers hated him because their father loved him more than the others and gave him a special coat of many colors. Moreover, it seems Joseph was guilty of some measure of pride in relating a couple of dreams in which his brothers and father symbolically bowed to him. The dreams fueled the brothers' jealousy, and they arranged to sell Joseph into slavery. What a lonely position he was in! He became the slave of Potiphar and quickly rose to a position of responsibility. Being alone in a foreign country he could easily have surrendered to temptation when Potiphar's wife tried to seduce him. However, he resisted her. She lied about the incident and Joseph again found himself in a desperate position. But Scripture records that the Lord was with Joseph.

We see here that the Lord's presence is the cure for any problem, including loneliness. After spending some time in prison Joseph had the opportunity to interpret a couple of dreams for Pharaoh and again Joseph rose to a position of high responsibility (second only to the Pharaoh).

Eventually a famine caused Joseph's brothers to seek food in Egypt, where they were reunited with him.

The Lord truly was with Joseph; in the end he was reunited with his father and brothers. We, too, need to remember that if we trust Christ, He is with us. He watches over every detail of our lives. Even in difficult times He is there and is working everything out for our good.

Job

Perhaps Job suffered more than any other individual in the Bible. The Book of Job vividly presents the problem of both physical and emotional pain. In fact, it even teaches that pain and suffering can actually help us to live more steadfastly for the Lord.

The Book of Job was written in order to give us an insight into the activity of Satan, the king of the sinful world. Though Job was subjected to much suffering by Satan, God revealed Himself even through that pain. The book demonstrates that it is possible for a person to maintain a full concentration on God even when the world around him seems to be collapsing.

From the opening lines of the Book of Job we know that he was a great and successful man. We are told that he was "blameless and upright, one who feared God, and turned away from evil" (Job 1:1 RSV). We also know that he was very wealthy, probably the richest man of his time. He was also a fine family man and was blessed with a vast amount of knowledge. No doubt Job enjoyed a peaceful life of contentment.

Here is where Satan entered the picture. Satan, always the skeptic, wanted to prove to God that the reason Job was so faithful to Him was that his life was so easy. So God, with His permissive will, allowed Satan to bring suffering upon Job to prove that a person truly dedicated to God would not succumb to sin. Satan tried several tactics to no avail. He began by wiping out Job's herds, he took away his servants, and even his sons and daughters. When all of this failed to cause Job to renounce his faith in God, Satan struck Job with disease. We do not know what the disease was, but from its biblical description it may have been leprosy or possibly elephantiasis. In any case, it was so serious that he was banished from the community, and he sat among the ashes outside the city gate.

Yet Job still refused to denounce God. Even his wife advised him to do so, yet we are told, "In all this Job did not sin with his lips" (Job 2:10 RSV). This is not to say that Job felt happy. In fact, there were moments when he wished he had never been born. He had lost his wealth, his children, his position in the town. His wife had turned against him. He was infected with the worst of diseases. Imagine the loneliness, the feeling of separation from all mankind. Yet, although he felt as low as a man can feel, he did not lose sight of the most important relationship of all.

Job had three friends who came to his side during this time of suffering, but they were of little help. Rather than offering comfort and support, they gave him ill-advised direction. Eventually their support of Job turned into condemnation, accusation, and sarcasm. Yet Job *still* clung to the truth that God is love and God is just. Though this truth made no sense to his friends, and though it seemingly was not borne out in his circumstances, Job was able to view life in proper perspective. He knew the temporary nature of suffering, relentless though it seemed. He knew that in the end God's love would be manifested.

And indeed, at the end of the book we are told that God did bless Job and relieve him from his suffering. In fact, God gave Job twice as much as he had formerly possessed. He had ten more children, and joy and happiness were once more a part of his life.

There is much comfort in the story of Job for those who have felt many lonely moments. This book illustrates that God will never allow Satan to bring us more pain and sorrow than we are capable of bearing. We may not always know God's reason for allowing us to suffer, but we are assured that God will always make available sufficient grace to help us overcome life's problems. We sometimes have the attitude that we deserve to have happiness and good fortune all the time. We can learn a lesson from Job, who stated, "The LORD gave, and the LORD has taken away; blessed be the name of the LORD" (Job 1:21 RSV).

Solomon

When we think of Solomon, several characteristics immediately come to mind. Foremost we think of Solomon as being one of the wisest men of all ages. We are told that the "whole earth sought the presence of Solomon to hear his wisdom, which God had put into his mind" (1 Kings 10:24 RSV). Distinguished from all other men by his tremendous intellect, he contributed greatly to the people of his day by being a master problem solver.

And his wisdom guides us even today by means of his biblical writings, for he is credited with writing a large share of the Book of Proverbs, which gives us practical insights into our daily walk with the Lord and with others.

We also know that Solomon, like Job, was an extremely wealthy man. We know that all of his drinking vessels were of gold not silver (1 Kings 10:21). His mansion was unbelievably elaborate. In fact, it was so huge and intricate in design that it took thirteen years to build (1 Kings 7:1).

One might think that Solomon with all of his wisdom and splendor rarely, if ever, had any personal problems. Yet he did. In fact, we know through his writings that Solomon was an intensely lonely and disillusioned man. As we look at some of the events in Solomon's life, it seems amazing that a man who possessed such wisdom and who was supposedly well-versed in knowledge of God could bring on himself such predicaments as to guarantee a lonely life.

Solomon's polygamy was virtually unrestrained, as he acquired one wife after another, many simply for reasons of political advantage. He condoned slavery and made use of it extensively for his own selfish gain. He aligned himself with foreign governments of questionable reputation. And in his old age, he backslid, even participating in idol worship. Overall it seems that Solomon frequently turned his back on his religious convictions for personal advancements.

While Solomon accumulated many remarkable possessions and the nation of Israel rose to a position of world prominence under him, he was not loved and adored as his father David had been. Solomon's taxation of his subjects was at times crippling. Concern for the individual citizen was lost in Solomon's zeal to build a glorious spectacle for others to envy. The result was his heavy use of slave labor. His passion for grandeur caused him to lose sight of the truly important things in life.

If, as is generally assumed, Solomon was the author of Ecclesiastes, he ended up a confused, disgusted man. The word *vanity*, which appears about forty times in the book, is Solomon's verdict regarding his life spent apart from God. Solomon wrote, "I have seen everything that is done under the sun; and behold, all is vanity and a striving after wind" (Eccles. 1:14 RSV).

Many biblical scholars believe that Ecclesiastes was written in Solomon's old age as he reflected on his life-long pursuit of happiness. While some people consider a wealthy existence filled with wine, women, and song to be the ultimate in living, Solomon eventually came to a different conclusion. Ecclesiastes reveals to us the empty and lonely heart of a sad old king. Certainly all is vanity for a person who lives a life chasing after earthly treasures yet neglecting to lay up for himself treasures in heaven.

Elijah

Today it is rather common to be under physical and mental stress, to become depressed (even suicidal), and to feel all alone. Such was the case with Elijah after his victory over the prophets of Baal on Mount Carmel. The story of Elijah's depression is found in 1 Kings 19:1–18:

> Now Ahab told Jezebel all that Elijah had done, and how he had killed all the prophets with the sword. Then Jezebel sent a messenger to Elijah, saying, "So may the

gods do to me and even more, if I do not make your life as the life of one of them by tomorrow about this time." And he was afraid and arose and ran for his life and came to Beersheba, which belongs to Judah, and left his servant there. But he himself went a day's journey into the wilderness, and came and sat down under a juniper tree; and he requested for himself that he might die, and said, "It is enough; now, O LORD, take my life, for I am not better than my fathers." And he lay down and slept under a juniper tree; and behold, there was an angel touching him, and he said to him, "Arise, eat." Then he looked and behold, there was at his head a bread cake baked on hot stones, and a jar of water. So he ate and drank and lay down again. And the angel of the LORD came again a second time and touched him and said, "Arise, eat, because the journey is too great for you." So he arose and ate and drank, and went in the strength of that food forty days and forty nights to Horeb, the mountain of God.

Then he came there to a cave, and lodged there; and behold, the word of the LORD came to him, and He said to him, "What are you doing here, Elijah?" And he said, "I have been very zealous for the LORD, the God of hosts; for the sons of Israel have forsaken Thy covenant, torn down Thine altars, and killed Thy prophets with the sword. And I alone am left; and they seek my life, to take it away." So He said, "Go forth, and stand on the mountain before the LORD." And behold, the LORD was passing by! And a great and strong wind was rending the mountains and breaking in pieces the rocks before the LORD; but the LORD was not in the wind. And after the wind an earthquake, but the LORD was not in the earthquake. And after the earthquake a fire, but the LORD was not in the fire; and after the fire a sound of a gentle blowing. And it came about when Elijah heard

> it, that he wrapped his face in his mantle, and went out and stood in the entrance of the cave. And behold, a voice came to him and said, "What are you doing here, Elijah?" Then he said, "I have been very zealous for the LORD, the God of hosts; for the sons of Israel have forsaken Thy covenant, torn down Thine altars and killed Thy prophets with the sword. And I alone am left; and they seek my life, to take it away."
>
> And the LORD said to him, "Go, return on your way to the wilderness of Damascus, and when you have arrived, you shall anoint Hazael king over Syria; and Jehu the son of Nimshi you shall anoint king over Israel; and Elisha the son of Shaphat of Abel-meholah you shall anoint as prophet in your place. And it shall come about, the one who escapes from the sword of Hazael, Jehu shall put to death, and the one who escapes from the sword of Jehu, Elisha shall put to death. Yet I will leave 7,000 in Israel, all the knees that have not bowed to Baal and every mouth that has not kissed him." (NASB)

Elijah was under stress (vv. 1–3). He was depressed (v. 4). He felt he was all alone in his love for the Lord (vv. 10, 14). It is very interesting to notice what God did:

God ministered to Elijah's physical needs for rest and food (vv. 5–8).

God showed Elijah His power (vv. 11–12).

God manifested Himself in a personal way to Elijah (vv. 12–13).

God let him ventilate his feelings (v. 14).

God gave him some specific duties to do (vv. 15–16).

God told him that he was not alone, that there were other believers. In fact, God said, "Yet I will leave

7,000 in Israel, all the knees that have not bowed to Baal and every mouth that has not kissed him" (v. 18).

When a depressed and lonely counselee comes to us today, we often give recommendations based on 1 Kings 19:

Take care of your physical needs. Get plenty of rest. Adopt a sensible, nutritious diet.

Reflect on Scripture passages that reveal the power of God. Consider that His tremendous strength is just as available today as it was to Elijah (a man subject to like passions as we are—James 5:17).

Spend a few minutes every day becoming more intimate with God. Meditate on verses that create a close, personal feeling with God; for example, Psalm 42:1: "As the deer pants for the water brooks, So my soul pants for Thee, O God" (NASB). Have a close walk with God.

Talk with God about your feelings and fears.

Plan specific daily activities that will further the cause of Christ. Get up, get busy. Be active.

Associate daily with other dedicated believers. Spend some time every day in meaningful interchange with other believers. Unite with other people.

Simon Peter

Simon Peter is one of the most diverse and colorful characters in the New Testament. We know him to be bold, easily angered, deeply spiritual, loyal, fearful, and powerfully persuasive. He was a doer. Certainly he was a man of many facets.

Simon Peter was given the name Simon at birth. At some point (perhaps as early as their first encounter—John 1:42) Jesus gave Simon the name Peter, meaning "rock" and emphasizing his steadfastness. When Peter made his bold declaration recognizing Jesus as the Son of God, Jesus said, "Blessed are you, Simon Barjona! For flesh and blood has not revealed this to you, but my Father who is in heaven. And I tell you, you are Peter, and on this rock I will build my church, and the powers of death shall not prevail against it" (Matt. 16:17–18 RSV).

In giving Simon the new name, Jesus was saying that He saw in Simon a new dimension. Throughout the New Testament we see Simon Peter as having two distinct personalities. One was a weak, self-centered man; the other a powerful, God-serving man. This serves as a reminder that because of sin even Christians will be prone to periods of weakness and suffering. In this life, Christianity is not a cure-all, but it gives us a means to do battle against our sinful tendencies.

Let's take a brief look at one of the most difficult moments in Simon Peter's life. When Jesus was arrested and sentenced to be crucified, the Jewish people felt vindictive toward those close to Him as well. After his Master had gone through the ordeal of the trial, Peter was afraid to identify himself as one who had been in Jesus' inner circle. When a maiden recognized him, he denied knowing Christ. When she pointed him out to some bystanders, he denied his relationship with Christ again. The bystanders were still convinced that he was a follower of Jesus; so he denied it yet a third time, with a curse (Mark 14:66–71).

Jesus had predicted earlier, against Simon Peter's protests, that this would happen. The disciple had been certain that he would never separate himself from Christ. When he realized his weakness in denying Christ, he broke down and wept (Mark 14:72). Certainly in the moments that followed, Simon Peter sunk to the depths of loneliness. He had betrayed God, his fellow disciples, and himself. He had allowed his selfish, sinful nature to take control.

The story of Simon Peter would be sad indeed if it ended with this experience. Yet at some point during the next few days, Peter came to his senses and reestablished a right relationship with God. When Jesus rose from the grave, Peter was one of the first two disciples to run to the tomb. The power of the Holy Spirit filled Peter to such an extent that he led a great revival that resulted in over three thousand professions of faith (Acts 2). He became a respected leader of the early church and was highly significant in the spread of the gospel.

Many of us have been at low points in our lives, as Simon Peter had been, feeling deeply ashamed of the way we have conducted our lives. Unfortunately, some do not rebound as Peter did. Some simply allow themselves to muddle in loneliness and self-degradation. Others give up trying to live right and turn to a life of corruption. We can learn from the life of Simon Peter. Although the influence of sin was still imbedded in him, he did not simply succumb. He determined to get on with the business of living a full life for his Lord. He did not allow his loneliness to become a disabling burden.

Thomas

When asked to describe the apostle Thomas, most people would use the word *doubting*. Perhaps it is unfair that Thomas has gone down in history tagged as the one who questioned whether Christ had actually risen from the grave. Actually, Thomas is not unlike many current believers who, at low moments in their lives, doubt the existence of God, or at least their own salvation through Jesus.

Although Thomas is not mentioned nearly as much as some of the other apostles, for example, Peter and John, we are given enough information to draw a few conclusions about his personality. Apparently, Thomas found it easy to look on the dark side of life, failing to keep in mind the long-range promises of Jesus. Distrust and pessimism were characteristic of Thomas. By nature he was demanding and would accept secondhand evidence from no one. He would probably not have described himself as a doubter but rather as a realist who must always live according to hard facts.

Three separate instances will reveal Thomas's nature. The first occurred when Jesus desired to go to the side of His good friends Mary and Martha when He heard their brother Lazarus had become seriously ill. The disciples, fearing that Jesus' enemies might try to seize Him, tried to talk Him out of making the trip. But when Jesus insisted, Thomas said to the rest, "Let us also go, that we may die with him" (John 11:16 RSV). In short, Thomas assumed that the worst would happen, forgetting how Jesus had handled His enemies in the past.

On another occasion Jesus was preparing His disciples for His death. He explained that He was leaving in order to prepare a place for His followers and that they knew the way where He was going. Until the end of time they would have the promise of Jesus' presence. But Thomas interrupted, saying, "Lord, we do not know where you are going; how can we know the way?" (John 14:5 RSV). Thomas was slow to accept any word, even from the Master, unless it was put in concrete terms.

The third incident, the most famous one, occurred after Jesus rose from the grave. For some reason Thomas had been absent when Christ presented Himself to His inner circle. A good guess is that Thomas was out wallowing in lonely despair. He refused to believe that Jesus had risen from the grave until he himself saw Jesus and placed his hand in His side.

Obviously, Thomas spent some confused and lonely moments questioning his relationship with Jesus and the rest of His followers. Like many of us today, he was caught up in skepticism and uncertainty regarding people in general, and Jesus Christ in particular. Perhaps we have been too harsh in our assessment of Thomas the doubter, for we, too, have known many moments of doubt. We must not be unfair in our view of Thomas. While he was pessimistic regarding Jesus' trip to see Mary, Martha, and Lazarus, he did go and encouraged the other disciples to go. While he was confused about Christ's mission on earth and His resurrection from death, he did stay with the group to satisfy his doubts. And after having many questions, he did make the greatest confession a person can make when he proclaimed Jesus "my Lord and my God" (John 20:28).

Whatever doubts Thomas had, whatever feelings of confusion and separation he suffered, we gain comfort from knowing that Thomas was able to rise above his weaknesses by confessing Jesus as his Lord and Savior.

And Jesus loved and accepted Thomas totally, just the way he was—doubts and all.

Paul

The most common advice people give when they are asked how to overcome loneliness is the obvious—unite with other people. The apostle Paul no doubt understood this, for in those passages in which he discusses growth in the local church he makes repeated references regarding how we are to deal with one another. He says that we are to be devoted to one another, to honor one another, to be of the same mind with one another, to accept one another, to admonish one another, to greet one another, to serve one another, to bear one another's burdens, to bear with one another, to submit to one another, to be members of one another, and to encourage one another—what potent cures for loneliness!

Considering the insight Paul had, it would be interesting to see what he did when confronted with loneliness. Second Timothy 4 is pertinent in this regard:

> I solemnly charge you in the presence of God and of Christ Jesus, who is to judge the living and the dead, and by His appearing and His kingdom: preach the word; be ready in season and out of season, reprove, rebuke, exhort, with great patience and instruction. For the time will come when they will not endure sound doctrine; but wanting to have their ears tickled, they will accumulate for themselves teachers in accordance to their own desires; and will turn away their ears from the truth, and will turn aside to myths. But you, be sober in all things,

endure hardship, do the work of an evangelist, fulfill your ministry. For I am already being poured out as a drink offering, and the time of my departure has come. I have fought the good fight, I have finished the course, I have kept the faith; in the future there is laid up for me the crown of righteousness, which the Lord, the righteous Judge, will award to me on that day; and not only to me, but also to all who have loved His appearing.

Make every effort to come to me soon; for Demas, having loved this present world, has deserted me and gone to Thessalonica; Crescens has gone to Galatia, Titus to Dalmatia. Only Luke is with me. Pick up Mark and bring him with you, for he is useful to me for service. But Tychicus I have sent to Ephesus. When you come bring the cloak which I left at Troas with Carpus, and the books, especially the parchments. Alexander the coppersmith did me much harm; the Lord will repay him according to his deeds. Be on guard against him yourself, for he vigorously opposed our teaching. At my first defense no one supported me, but all deserted me; may it not be counted against them. But the Lord stood with me, and strengthened me, in order that through me the proclamation might be fully accomplished, and that all the Gentiles might hear; and I was delivered out of the lion's mouth. The Lord will deliver me from every evil deed, and will bring me safely to His heavenly kingdom; to Him be the glory forever and ever. Amen.

Greet Prisca and Aquila, and the household of Onesiphorus. Erastus remained at Corinth, but Trophimus I left sick at Miletus. Make every effort to come before winter. Eubulus greets you, also Pudens and Linus and Claudia and all the brethren.

The Lord be with your spirit. Grace be with you. (NASB)

We would do well to follow Paul's example when we face lonely and difficult times:

Paul gave Timothy advice on how to carry out the work of evangelism (vv. 1–6). The implication is that Paul also continued ministering to others in this way as best he could.

Paul always had a purpose. He was aware that his work was in effect a fight (v. 7).

He asked his friend Timothy to come to see him (v. 9).

Paul honestly faced the fact that some of his friends had forsaken him (vv. 10, 16).

He kept providing for his intellectual and spiritual needs. The parchments he asked for (v. 13) were in all likelihood the Scriptures.

He encouraged himself with the knowledge that the Lord had always stood with him and strengthened him (v. 17).

He gave specific encouragement to other individuals.

We have taken a close look at seven Bible characters who experienced loneliness. There are many others we could cite. We can rest assured, then, that we are not alone in struggling with loneliness and personal failures. In fact, even God the Father feels lonely, for He desires to have fellowship with us. "For the eyes of the Lord search back and forth across the whole earth, looking for people whose hearts are perfect toward him" (2 Chron. 16:9 LB). Even though He has fellowship with the angels and perfect communion with the Holy Spirit and Christ, He longs for intimacy with you and me.

FOURTEEN

A FINAL THOUGHT

WE SINCERELY HOPE and trust that this book will have a beneficial effect on thousands of lives. If it is to succeed, however, the reader must regard it as more than a how-to manual. We presented the material as we did in order to help the reader gain a broad understanding of loneliness—not only its cures, but its causes and consequences as well. In order to confront a problem, we must first know exactly what we are dealing with. Just as it helps an army general to know and understand the movements of the enemy, it can be of great aid for us to comprehend the complexities of our emotional problems before we try to tackle them.

Many people ask us how to quit feeling lonely, or how to quit feeling depressed. They expect that by putting a prescribed plan of action into practice, the problem areas will just disappear. Well, it simply is not that easy. We humans are a lot more complicated than that. A set of instructions will often help fix a broken machine, but the human machine needs more than pat answers. This does not mean that we should discount good advice when it is given. Rather, it means that often we need a philosophical grip on life's problems.

We have seen many examples of individuals who, in struggling with emotional problems, were *not* given all the answers by a wise old sage yet were able to find the proper solutions anyway. That is, when people with motivation gain insights into their subtle emotional conflicts, they are sometimes capable of mapping out the best strategy for themselves. Some people already know the answers (the how-to's) to their problems. What they need is to recognize how their problems have been perpetuated by inappropriate thought patterns and inaccurate conceptions of the most basic truths of life.

In asserting that loneliness is a problem that can be overcome, there is one final point we wish to make—the human *will* is more powerful than human *emotions*. If a person determines to release himself from the control of nagging emotions, *it can happen*. Notice that we are not saying that we can simply get rid of our emotions. It is evident from the preceding pages that because of sin humans will always feel a measure of loneliness. But we do not have to be *controlled* by this emotion or by any other emotion for that matter. We cannot totally eliminate the presence of negative emotions. But we can learn to be in control of our negative emotions, rather than letting them be in control of us!

There is a great encouragement to be found in Philippians 4:13: "I can do all things through Him who strengthens me" (NASB). We sometimes have difficulty being patient with people who persistently say, "I can't."

What they mean is, "I won't," or, "I choose not to," or, "I do not know how." When a person takes the "I can" attitude, it is more than likely that he will be able to do what he sets out to do.

Determination, with faith in God, to overcome life's problems is the key to success. Often we feel we will not be successful and therefore do not determine to be successful. But according to Scripture, a sense of determination can help overpower our negative feelings. If we allow ourselves to be guided strictly by feelings, we could be in big trouble. However, if we adopt an attitude of responsible determination based on biblical truths, while still listening carefully to our feelings as well, we stand a good chance to be genuine successes.

We would not want to be accused of minimizing the heartfelt painful emotions that people experience. Feelings are not to be ignored. We certainly understand when a person feels lonely. In this day and age, we all have problems that can seem bigger than life. Yet, if there is any truth at all to the Scriptures (and we believe the Scriptures to be inerrant), we can heave a great sigh of relief to know that there is hope for our problems if we put God's principles into practice. Putting God's principles into practice will make the difference between being disappointed that this book has not cured your loneliness and being pleased that it has helped to bring greater intimacy and less loneliness.

NOTES

Chapter 7: The Victims of Loneliness—from Young to Old

1. Robert S. Weiss, ed., *The Experience of Loneliness: Studies in Emotional and Social Isolation* (Cambridge, Mass.: M.I.T. Press, 1973), 23–25.

2. Rubin Zick, "Seeking a Cure for Loneliness," *Psychology Today* (October 1979): 82–90.

Chapter 12: Do Something about It!

1. Adapted from Paul Meier and Richard Meier, *Family Foundations: How to Have a Happy Home* (Grand Rapids: Baker, 1981), 61–62.

2. For an explanation of how to deal with anger biblically, see ibid., 46–60.

Les Carter, Ph.D., is associated with the Minirth Clinic in Richardson, Texas. He is specially trained in the treatment of emotional adjustments and relationship problems. In addition to his counseling practice, Dr. Carter has appeared on hundreds of radio and television broadcasts and conducts conferences on the relationship between spirituality and psychology.

Paul Meier is a Christian physician and psychiatrist with the Paul Meier New Life Clinic in Richardson, Texas. He has conducted seminars throughout the United States on counseling and child-rearing.

Frank Minirth is a Christian psychiatrist and founder of the Minirth Clinic in Richardson, Texas. He is the author or coauthor of over thirty books, including *Happiness Is a Choice* and the *Choosing to Forgive* workbook.